STUDENT UNIT GUIDE

A2 Economics

UNIT 8

OCR

Module 2888: Economics in a European Context

John Hearn

Philip Allan Updates
Market Place
Deddington
Oxfordshire
OX15 0SE

tel: 01869 338652
fax: 01869 337590
e-mail: sales@philipallan.co.uk
www.philipallan.co.uk

ISBN 0 86003 678 2

This Guide has been written specifically to support students preparing for the OCR A2 Economics Unit 8 examination. The content has been neither approved nor endorsed by OCR and remains the sole responsibility of the author.

Printed by Information Press, Eynsham, Oxford

Contents

Introduction

Content Guidance

Questions and Answers

Introduction

This module will be the last one studied to complete the OCR A-level specification. It is the most important A2 module, carrying 40% of the overall marks and 20% of all the marks allocated to the A-level. In the words of the examining board:

> It should be recognised from the outset that the content of all AS modules will be further examined through synoptic assessment in the terminal Unit 2888: 'Economics in a European Context'.

All A-level boards are required to include a minimum of 20% synoptic assessment, and all the questions in this module are of that nature. More precisely, a synoptic paper requires candidates to understand the various connections between economic theory and the real world. In this module, concepts, theories and hypotheses are to be applied to economic issues and problems in an evaluative and analytical way, all wrapped up inside a European context. Here, Europe includes the countries of what was originally referred to as:

- western Europe
- eastern Europe

Western Europe now includes a broad division between the 15 countries which make up the European Union (EU) and the non-EU countries, which include Switzerland, Norway and Iceland. Within the EU countries there is also an important division between the 12 countries that comprise the euro zone and have accepted the single currency, and the three countries — UK, Denmark and Sweden — which are not part of the euro zone.

Eastern Europe is now split into two broad divisions. What was originally the USSR has become the Commonwealth of Independent States (CIS), and the former satellite countries of the USSR have been grouped together as the Independent States of Central and Eastern Europe (CEE).

It is important to remember that any question that refers to Europe may require you to include all these broad European groupings. Marks will be lost by those students who refer only to the EU or western Europe or euro zone countries.

In this synoptic unit the aim is to take all the AS knowledge referred to in the OCR Approved Specifications as 'the economist's tool kit' of concepts, theories and techniques', and test your ability to use this knowledge in a European context. This means that, although you may be directed to focus your attention on the real world, a descriptive answer that does not use economic theory will score very few, if any, marks.

Almost the first question to ask yourself when you approach a new topic in the course or read a question in the examination is: 'What economic theory can be usefully applied to this situation?'

Common themes that are likely to be addressed in this module are:

- the advantages and disadvantages of a single market for European Union countries
- an evaluation of economic and monetary union (EMU) and the single European currency
- whether the UK should join the single European currency
- the strengths and significant weaknesses of the Common Agricultural Policy
- the advantages and disadvantages of factor mobility throughout EU countries
- the problems faced by the transitional economies of Europe
- inequality throughout Europe
- an evaluation of the 'new Europe'

Pre-issued case study materials

The way in which you study this module is very different from the way you study the rest of A-level economics. Six or seven weeks before you sit the examination, you will be issued with stimulus material. This may include articles from *Economic Review*, bank reviews, newspapers and other periodicals and occasional papers from various organisations. It may also include sets of statistical data. The factual content of the knowledge required in the examination will be incorporated in the pre-issued material. Although you will not be able to carry notes or any of the case study material into the examination, you will be provided with a clean set of material along with an unseen question paper.

After the case study material has been issued, and before the examination, the sensible approach as you familiarise yourself with the content is to ask yourself (and your teacher) what economic theory learnt in the AS part of the course is directly relevant to what you are currently reading. Although you should not place too much reliance on question-spotting, it would be foolish not to try to anticipate the questions that are likely to be asked and prepare notes on these inspired guesses. For example, if an article is about price elasticity of demand for various products in Europe, or about market failure in a certain industry, or about free trade as opposed to protection, then the focus of a significant part of your work is set.

How to use this guide

This introduction explains the difference between the synoptic unit and all the other units studied to complete the AS and full A-level. It is necessary to grasp this difference from the very start so that you do not involve yourself in unnecessary work but focus clearly on the essential elements required to be successful in this examination.

The second part of this guide, Content Guidance, offers a broad overview of Module 2888: 'Economics in a European Context' and its four main areas of study:

- background knowledge
- the 'new Europe'
- the single European market and economic and monetary union
- the transition economies of Europe

For each study area, there is a clear statement regarding the skills that must be developed. By the time of the examination, you must have learnt the definitions of a number of key words and be able to understand certain concepts, hypotheses and theories, many of which are drawn from the AS specifications.

An attempt has been made to highlight the most relevant parts from the units already studied, but remember that you may be questioned on any part of the AS specifications. Understanding on its own is not enough, so the Content Guidance also identifies the things you need to be able to explain, analyse, apply and evaluate within a European context in order to achieve a high grade.

The third part of this guide, Questions and Answers, includes three sets of case study materials equivalent to those that would be pre-issued by the examining board. Following this are the three related examination papers, which include questions, a mark scheme, a grade-A answer and a list of potential errors and omissions that students might make.

Below is a list of recommendations for the use of the case study materials and the examination papers.

(1) If possible, give yourself up to 2 weeks to complete the preparation (from the case study material) before attempting each practice paper. Do not look at the practice questions until you are ready to complete them under timed conditions.

(2) Read through the articles and statistics, making brief notes as you go. Satisfy yourself that you understand what the statistics are showing. Look at the diagrams and take note of what is included on each axis and the trends and breaks in trends that are shown. Add your own narrative to the diagrams.

(3) Next, read through your notes and the articles once again. Ask yourself which economic theories from your course are relevant and can be applied to what you are reading. Write out a list of questions that you consider likely to be included in the examination paper. Practise answering the questions you have identified.

(4) When you feel fully prepared, set aside 1 hour 45 minutes to complete the paper without being interrupted. It is important to observe strictly the examination timings so that you familiarise yourself with how much can be achieved in 1 hour 45 minutes. Be guided in the time you spend on each question by the mark allocation given at the end. One of the major causes of underachievement is not allocating the required time, particularly to the last question.

(5) When you have completed the examination paper, use the mark scheme to help you to mark your script. This is a useful exercise — giving yourself the examiner's job will focus your attention on what is and what is not important. Remember, it is quality and not quantity that counts. A rough guide to the marks associated with each grade is as follows:

Grade A	80%+	Grade D	50–59%
Grade B	70–79%	Grade E	40–49%
Grade C	60–69%		

(6) Finally, compare your answer with the relevant grade-A answer. Remember, this answer is not perfect, although it should be taken as a sound guide to a top grade.

Carefully read the examiner comments that appear after each section of the grade-A answer: these offer useful hints. Then, in order to check whether you fell into any of the traps commonly made by students, read through the 'potential errors and omissions'.

Assessment objectives

The aim of stimulus material is to *stimulate* your thought processes and encourage you to think like an economist. The questions on the examination paper will be based on this material, but you will not be able to answer the questions by simply regurgitating what is in the case studies. There are, then, three skills required in this module:

(1) Understanding of the pre-issued material.

(2) Knowledge of which theories, techniques and concepts from your AS notes are relevant.

(3) The ability to express this understanding as an economist in continuous prose.

The examining board separates the assessment objectives into four skill levels. These are illustrated in the table below, using the example of a customs union.

Assessment objective	Skills	Percentage of total mark
Level 1	The ability to understand and express knowledge of the specification content, e.g. the ability to write out a definition of a customs union.	20%
Level 2	The ability to apply this knowledge and understanding critically to real and simulated situations, e.g. the ability to explain the extent to which the European Union is a customs union and explain the situation it replaced and how it differs from other economic unions.	20%
Level 3	The ability to use economic principles to analyse the situation, e.g. using a supply and demand diagram to show how trade creation and trade diversion occur when a customs union is set up.	30%
Level 4	The ability to reflect upon economic arguments, apply economic theory to European issues, evaluate evidence and make informed judgements as an economist, e.g. is the European Union functioning as a customs union, and what effects are the Common Agricultural Policy and the single European currency having upon this economic union?	30%

It is important to note that the assessment objectives for A2 modules are weighted heavily towards levels 3 and 4, whereas the AS papers have a 20% weighting on levels 3 and 4 and a 30% weighting on levels 1 and 2.

There are quality of language marks included in the mark scheme for each question. In a question worth 20 marks, approximately 3 marks will be set aside for quality of written communication. The OCR Approved Specifications state that all the quality of language marks will be achieved when:

> Complex ideas are expressed clearly and fluently, using a style of writing appropriate to the complex subject matter. Sentences and paragraphs, consistently relevant, are well structured, using specialist technical terminology where appropriate. There are few, if any, errors of spelling, punctuation and grammar.

This means that if you finish the examination paper with a few minutes to go before 'time up', you should re-read your answer and tidy up the quality of your writing.

Planning your work and preparing a revision strategy

- Familiarise yourself with the specification content included in the AS modules
  Module 2881 — The Market System
  Module 2882 — Market Failure and Government Intervention
  Module 2883 — The National and International Economy
- From the start of the course, read a quality newspaper and extract all the relevant articles about the economics of Europe.
- Listen to current affairs programmes and news programmes and be prepared to write down relevant points about the new Europe, the single European market (SEM), economic and monetary union (EMU) and the transition economies of Europe.
- Read the relevant articles in *Economic Review* (including back copies), published four times a year by Philip Allan Updates. Also, read current bank reviews.
- The internet provides a range of websites from which information about Europe can be gathered. Any search engine can be a useful starting-point. Some useful websites are listed below:
  www.bankofengland.co.uk
  www.hm-treasury.gov.uk/press
  www.ecb.int (European Central Bank)
  www.worldbank.org (for worldwide data and maps)
  www.census.gov/main/www.stat_int.html (a list of international agencies that provide statistics)
  www.un.org (follow the links through 'text version' to 'Cyber School Bus' and 'InfoNation' among a choice of other useful sites)

  Libraries that receive *The Economist* can take advantage of a free subscription to the internet edition, which includes a searchable archive of past articles.
- Be prepared to start work on the pre-issued case study material as soon as it arrives, in the way described on page 5 of this introduction.
- The assessment objectives are weighted heavily to the higher-level skills, so always try to take your preparatory work up to these levels. Level 3 will often use the following words:

Account for... Consider...
Analyse... Explain...
Apply... Justify...
Compare...

while level 4 will often use:

Assess... Discuss...
Comment... Evaluate
Criticise... To what extent...?

- As early as possible, find out the date of your examination so that you can prepare a revision strategy. You should include a stock of time that can be used if any emergency should arise.
- Avoid the tendency to revise the material you already know and to ignore the more difficult parts of the course. It is reasonable to assume that the aspects you find difficult are going to appear in the examination as a test of higher-level skills.
- The process of organisation, preparation and revision that goes on throughout the course will have rooted some content firmly in your long-term memory. Over the last few weeks, help your short-term memory to upload the final details by using acronyms to remember lists, patterns to remember links and key words to trigger a series of associated points.
- If time allows, allocate several weeks to work on each of the three practice examination papers included in this guide.

Useful references

The main textbook for this module and the three modules of AS economics is *Economics for AS*, edited by Colin Bamford and published by Cambridge University Press, 2000. Chapters 11–13 cover this A2 module.

Hearn, J. (2000) *OCR Economics AS Unit 1 Student Unit Guide, Module 2881: The Market System*, Philip Allan Updates.

Westaway, T. (2000) *OCR Economics AS Unit 2 Student Unit Guide, Module 2882: Market Failure and Government Intervention*, Philip Allan Updates.

Hearn, J. (2000) *OCR Economics AS Unit 3 Student Unit Guide, Module 2883: The National and International Economy*, Philip Allan Updates.

Hearn, J. (2000) *AS/A-level Economics Essential Word Dictionary*, Philip Allan Updates. This includes all the important definitions and terms referred to in the module specifications.

Hearn, J. (2000) *AS/A-level Exam Revision Notes*, Philip Allan Updates. This covers all the basic economic theory used throughout the AS/A-level courses.

Other books to dip into include:

Dyker, D. A. (1999) *The European Economy* (2nd edn), Longman.

Healey, N. M. (1995) *The Economics of the New Europe*, Routledge.

Levigne, M. (1999) *The Economics of Transition* (2nd edn), Macmillan.

Content Guidance

This section of the guide outlines the background knowledge that is assumed to be in place as part of the synoptic element of this module. It also summarises the three topic areas to which this background knowledge will have to be applied:

- the 'new Europe'
- the single European market and economic and monetary union
- the transition economies of Europe

Background knowledge

Because it is synoptic, this examination can test any of the content included under the three compulsory modules that make up the AS course. The OCR specification states that this module will require synoptic knowledge of:

- competitive markets and how they work
- the different market structures, e.g. monopoly
- economic efficiency within market structures
- market imperfections and market failure
- the role of government intervention in markets
- the macroeconomic performance of the economy
- processes and policies in macroeconomics
- international trade and protection

The 'new Europe'

Europe today is very different from Europe 20 years ago. This component of the module requires a historical perspective on the developments that have taken place, particularly during the 1990s. It is necessary to understand the political decision-making structure overlying the economic structures that have been put in place throughout Europe, and to ask yourself the questions:

- Are they efficient?
- Are they performing as expected?
- How do they compare with structures found in other parts of the global economy?

The single European market (SEM) and economic and monetary union (EMU)

This part of the course is specifically about the European Union (EU). It will be necessary to evaluate the extent to which the EU has evolved from a customs union to a single market with monetary union. Has the removal of barriers to trade allowed comparative advantage to function and gains from trade to take place? Will the UK join the single European currency and do the advantages of EMU outweigh the disadvantages?

The transition economies of Europe

This section looks at those economies of Europe which started as a centrally planned group under the trading monopoly of COMECON and considers their reasonably abrupt transition to competitive market economies. Some of these countries are now looking forward to integration with the EU.

Background knowledge

Although it is possible that any of the AS economic theory can be tested in this module, the pre-issued case study will give you direction towards the most likely topics for inclusion in the examination.

For example, if the case study includes articles about specific marketplaces in Europe, then supply and demand analysis, market clearing prices, degrees of competition, shifts and movements in the representative curves and elasticities may be tested.

It is advisable to read through all the case study materials and highlight the underlying economic theory that is referred to or is implicit within what has been written. Then go back to your AS notes and make sure all the relevant theory is understood. The examining board has made it quite clear that it wants to test whether you can think like an economist and apply the concepts, hypotheses and theories you have learnt in the compulsory modules effectively.

Essential terms

Each of the AS Unit Guides in this series contains comprehensive lists of essential terms. Below is a brief list of the most essential 'essential terms'.

- aggregate demand
- aggregate supply
- balance of payments
- comparative advantage
- consumer surplus
- contestable market
- cost–benefit analysis
- diseconomies of scale
- economic efficiency
- economic growth (the)
- economic problem
- economies of scale
- elasticity
- exchange rate
- externalities
- fiscal policy
- gains from trade
- market failure
- merit goods
- monetary policy
- monopolistic competition
- monopoly
- multiplier
- opportunity cost
- private goods
- productive factors
- profit
- public goods

Understanding

You will need to understand the following:

- how competitive markets clear their products
- what is meant by market imperfection and market failure
- what makes a market efficient or inefficient
- why governments intervene in markets
- the main components of aggregate demand and aggregate supply
- the policies used in macroeconomic management
- the reasoning behind free international trade and protected trade

Explanation

You will need to be able to explain the following:

- why real markets are not perfect and how their efficiency can be increased
- the various market structures that best describe the markets of the real world, e.g. monopolistic competition, oligopoly, monopoly and contestable markets
- the mechanisms of, and the differences between, monetary and fiscal policy
- the process of international trade and the types of barrier that can be used to restrict free trade

Analysis

You will need to be able to analyse the following:

- the relationship between price and quantity demanded or supplied, the relationship between income and quantity demanded, and how these relationships can be measured using elasticity
- how economies can be represented by the aggregate supply/aggregate demand model, and how the model can be used to illustrate changes in economic activity through shifts and movements in the representative curves
- the factors which affect exchange rates and the impact exchange rate changes have on an economy
- the cause and effect of inflation, unemployment, balance of payments problems and slow or fast economic growth

Evaluation

You will need to be able to evaluate a wide range of issues across Europe, using your economist's tool kit. The set reading will provide you with direction, while some of the possible topics that may be chosen are outlined below:

- The Common Agricultural Policy (CAP) of the European Union was introduced to deal with market imperfections in the agricultural industry, but is now used by many economists to illustrate market failure on a grand scale. Nevertheless, it is one of the most important reasons why countries outside the union are seeking membership.
- Inequalities of income, wealth and living standards throughout Europe are considerable, particularly when western Europe is compared with the transition economies of eastern Europe.
- There are considerable differences within the European Union, as well as between the other countries of Europe, in their rates of growth, inflation and levels of unemployment.

Check points

Be aware of the following:

- It is an all too common mistake of many students, faced with a real world issue, to forget economic theory and give a superficial, descriptive answer. For example, a question about minimum price guarantees in the CAP must trigger the thought processes of an economist, who will start by assuming a theoretical market for an agricultural product with assumed demand, supply and equilibrium conditions. Superimposed on this market model can be minimum price guarantees that have no effect on the market if they are below the market clearing price. This explains why some products are unaffected by minimum price guarantees. However, if the guaranteed price is above the equilibrium price, there is likely to be a considerable distortion in the form of a surplus of products that cannot be sold.

- A rough rule of thumb before answering any question on this paper is to ask yourself: 'What is the underlying theory relevant to this issue?'
- When the question is about Europe, do not confine your answer to the European Union. Remember there are countries in western, central and eastern Europe that do not belong to the EU.

The 'new Europe'

After the Second World War, the first real attempt to bring about a degree of economic integration throughout western Europe was the establishment, through the 1957 Treaty of Rome, of the European Economic Community (EEC) as a customs union of six members — Belgium, France, Germany, Holland, Italy and Luxembourg. The UK joined in 1973, along with Denmark and Ireland. They were followed by Greece (1981), Portugal and Spain (1986) and Austria, Sweden and Finland (1995).

Soon after its inception, the EEC started to develop a uniform approach to a whole range of economic, social, legal and political criteria. By 1993, the EEC had established the structure for a single European market. It was renamed the European Union (EU) and, under the Maastricht Treaty, established the framework for a more federal Europe with its own currency, the euro. Not all countries (the UK among them) adopted the euro in January 1999, but it is anticipated that all EU member countries will join sooner or later.

The process of integration has produced the biggest trading bloc in the global economy. It has the largest consumer market in the world and accounts for approximately 40% of all exports. Integration has meant the blurring of national boundaries as tariffs have been removed, quotas have been abolished and non-tariff barriers have been tackled. Government policies on taxation, expenditure, exchange rates, transport, legislation and defence are being harmonised, and productive factors are allowed to move freely throughout the EU.

Essential terms

- customs union
- euro
- European Central Bank
- European Economic Community
- European Union
- excise duty
- free-trade area
- Maastricht Treaty

- quotas
- single European currency
- single European market
- tariffs
- taxation
- Treaty of Rome

Understanding

You will need to understand the following:

- how the 'new Europe' has evolved in general over the last 50 years, and in particular over the last 10 years
- how decision-making and implementation take place within the European Union
- the changes that may take place, and are currently taking place, including the anticipated increase in the membership of the EU as more countries agree to be bound by the 'Copenhagen criteria' (established in 1993 to assess the readiness of the transition economies to join the EU)

Explanation

You will need to be able to explain the following:

- the nature, meaning and levels of economic integration between member states and the aims of promoting the free movement of products and productive factors, so increasing efficiency and accelerating economic growth
- the harmonisation of the political process and the development of supranational organisations such as the European Central Bank
- the nature of free-trade areas, customs unions and other economic unions, highlighting their main differences

Analysis

You will need to be able to analyse the following:

- the various tax systems used in member countries
- the advantages and disadvantages of national currencies compared with a single European currency
- the main differences that still exist between member countries

Evaluation

You will need to be able to evaluate the following:

- the degree to which convergence may or may not be considered important
- the various levels of economic integration and why the underlying theory does not always produce the desired outcome in reality

Check points

Be aware of the following:

- The 'new Europe' includes many countries that are not members of the EU, so do not restrict your answer to parts of the new Europe unless clearly directed.
- Remember that both in the past and in the present there are various types of integration throughout Europe, including:

— common markets
— customs unions
— economic union
— free-trade areas
— monetary union
— single markets

The single European market (SEM) and economic and monetary union (EMU)

Gradually, the European Union developed out of the customs union that was the EEC. This group of nations created a large market for their countries' producers with no internal trade barriers and a common external tariff barrier. As the group of nations has become larger, so a loose trading alliance has grown into the single European market which boasts that its frontiers have been removed and that there is complete freedom of movement throughout the member states for people and products.

The economic union means common commercial laws, an alignment of technical standards and quality control underpinned by a converging legal and tax structure. In reality, the situation is not quite as envisaged by the Single European Act, although member countries have moved a long way towards harmonisation. However, it is still not advisable to try to travel through the EU without a passport, and people can still expect to be held up at national frontiers.

Many people consider the final step towards a single market will be the acceptance of monetary union in which the euro becomes the legal tender of all member countries.

Essential terms

- convergence criteria
- economic and monetary union (EMU)
- economic sovereignty
- European monetary system (EMS)
- factor mobility
- national debt
- price transparency
- Single European Act
- Social Charter
- trade creation
- trade diversion

Understanding

You will need to understand the following:

- the characteristics and structure of a single European market that has removed all tariff and non-tariff barriers

- what is meant by economic and monetary union
- the law of comparative advantage

Explanation

You will need to be able to explain the following:

- how the application of the law of comparative advantage can produce gains from trade
- developments in the European monetary system
- the importance of convergence criteria to the success of the single European currency
- the main changes that are taking place in trade throughout Europe as the result of integration and current global developments

Analysis

You will need to be able to analyse the following:

- the comparative statistics and information that can be used to compare the European Union with other global economic unions
- the immediate (static) effects of integration and the likely changes that will take place over time (dynamic)
- how the process of interaction has affected the mobility of labour (e.g. Premiership football teams) and capital
- the process of trade creation and trade diversion when a customs union is established, using the figure below

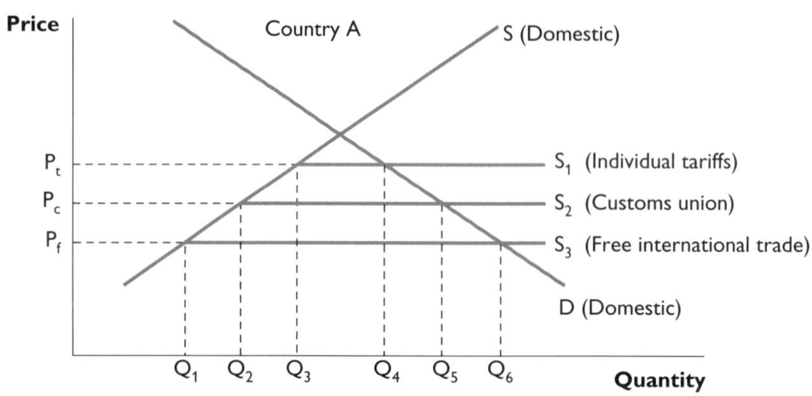

If there is no international trade, equilibrium in country A is represented by the intersection of S and D.

P_t

If international trade takes place and all countries have their own individual tariffs in place, the supply curve will become perfectly elastic at P_t.

P_c

If a customs union with a lower common external tariff is introduced, trade will be diverted from country A's domestic producers (Q_3–Q_2), net trade creation will occur between Q_4 and Q_5 and imports will be Q_5–Q_2.

P_f

If there were free international trade, more domestic production would be diverted to importers (Q_2–Q_1) and there would be further net trade creation (Q_5–Q_6).

The figure above illustrates that a customs union is likely to lead to net trade creation when compared to a situation of countries with their own tariffs. However, compared with free international trade, it is likely to be a second-best solution.

Evaluation

You will need to be able to evaluate the following:

- the costs and benefits of a single European currency
- the costs and benefits of establishing a customs union
- the reality of integration compared with the underlying economic theory
- the likely developments in the future as the countries of the European Union push for closer economic and monetary integration
- the implications to countries of full integration (in terms of economic and monetary union), partial integration (e.g. where the UK has not agreed to adopt the euro) and no integration (where some countries have decided to stay outside the EU)

Check points

- Remember that less than half the countries in Europe are members of the single European market; therefore, be careful not to confuse the 'ins' with the 'outs'.
- Remember that to benefit from trade a country does not need an absolute advantage in the production of any product. As long as it has a comparative advantage, this is sufficient to produce trade gains through specialisation. Comparative advantage exists when the opportunity costs of producing a particular product are lower in one country than in another.
- Because countries are likely to have significant tariff barriers before they consider joining a customs union, the whole process will be a step towards freer trade and the effect will be one of net trade creation.

The transition economies of Europe

For much of the last century Europe was a continent of two extremes. In western Europe there were countries that had embraced the market to a greater or lesser extent and relied upon the price mechanism to allocate products and productive factors.

The means of production could be privately owned and the rewards, through ownership, in the form of rent, interest, profits and dividends, could be reaped by individuals. In contrast, eastern Europe comprised countries whose economies were centrally planned. The allocation of products and productive factors was centrally directed, and property rights over the means of production were held by the state. Rewards to people were based upon a perception of their needs rather than in response to their economic effort.

This division was particularly well illustrated on either side of the Berlin Wall: western Europeans saw their standards of living rising significantly after the Second World War, while their counterparts on the eastern side of the wall saw their living standards frozen and the gap between them and their close neighbours growing increasingly larger.

At the end of the 1980s the strains of trying to plan and manage command economies finally gave way, and 25 independent countries set off down the road towards capitalism in search of freedom of choice, private property and the financial rewards that could be achieved through a successful private enterprise. They were loosely grouped into the former countries of the USSR, which made up the Commonwealth of Independent States (CIS), and the other independent states of Central and Eastern Europe (CEE).

The road from command economy to capitalist economy has been particularly difficult. Not only has there been a steep learning curve for consumers and producers, but there has also been the significant problem of dismantling an economic system that had resources and skills in the wrong place, and a mismatch between supply and demand that would take time to alleviate. In the communist revolution it had been relatively easy to take away private property rights, but it was much more difficult to return them in an equitable way.

Throughout eastern Europe there were significant differences in the inheritance that each country took into the period of transition. Some countries had significantly more markets in place, albeit markets that were not officially recognised under communism. Land resources varied from country to country as did population size, growth potential and living standards. Financial markets were almost non-existent. Currencies were unstable and unable to be traded on foreign exchange markets. Trade needed to be liberalised and firms needed to look outside Comecon (Council for Mutual Economic Aid) towards western Europe and the rest of the world.

Privatising a few state-run firms in western Europe has had its problems, but privatising a whole country is creating potentially damaging and destabilising costs of transition.

Essential terms

- black economy
- capitalism
- Central Bank
- command economy
- common property rights
- financial intermediation

- inflation
- private property rights
- privatisation
- sustainable economic growth
- trade liberalisation
- transition economy
- unemployment

Understanding

You will need to understand the following:

- the historical context within which the command economy was seen as a more equitable way of allocating resources than the uncaring 'invisible hand'
- the gradual realisation that the command economies were not producing the growth rates and living standards of the market-orientated economies
- the timescale over which the former command economies of central and eastern Europe are moving towards free market capitalism

Explanation

You will need to be able to explain the following:

- the nature and main characteristics of a command economy, in which the absence of private property rights and the presence of central planning and direction have replaced the price system as an allocative mechanism
- the inherent weaknesses of an economic system that plans to allocate resources to satisfy the perceived individual and collective needs of millions of people
- the variety of economic reforms that have been put in place to kickstart and maintain the transition to a market economy
- the internal and external trade liberalisation, the introduction of modern financial markets and the adoption of macroeconomic management both to stabilise the economy and to create a framework for faster economic growth

Analysis

You will need to be able to analyse the following:

- the difference between the problems and inefficiencies of central planning and the problems associated with the process of transition to a market economy
- the economic performance of the command economies before and during the transition process and how they compare with the other economies of western Europe
- the economic inefficiency, including both the productive and allocative inefficiency, that existed, considering the near-monopoly structures created within Comecon

Evaluation

You will need to be able to evaluate the following:

- the transitional process which has been referred to as 'shock therapy', compared with the 'gradualism' that has been preferred by some countries
- the foreseeable problems and prospects for integrating the CIS and CEE countries into the European Union

- the costs and benefits and likely success of a transition from a centrally controlled economy to a market economy
- the reasons why some of the transitional economies are pushing hard to be accepted within the EU, and the advantages and disadvantages to the EU of their eventual inclusion

Check points

- When you are answering a question about the advantages and disadvantages of command and market economies, remember that the costs involved in transition may play a significant part in determining the outcome.
- It is important to note that, although the command economies of eastern and central Europe were superficially similar, there were considerable underlying differences. It is these differences that are creating a variety of approaches and diverse responses to the process of transition.

Questions & Answers

In this section of the guide there are three samples of pre-issued case study materials and three examination papers, each followed by a mark scheme, a sample grade-A answer and a list of potential problems.

Pre-issued case study materials

The pre-issued materials are separated from the relevant examination paper so that you are not tempted to look at the questions as you read through the case studies. Articles and statistics similar to these will be pre-issued 6 or 7 weeks before the exam, and it is important to use the practice materials in this guide as if you are preparing for a real examination. You will not be allowed to take the materials into the examination, but a clean set will be provided with the examination paper.

Questions

In the examination, all the questions are compulsory and the time allocated for answering them is 1 hour 45 minutes. The questions can be drawn from theory and practice that was introduced throughout the AS specification as well as common themes that can be tested in either of the A2 optional papers. The examination will test the range of assessment objectives, with a weighting on the higher-level skills of application, analysis and evaluation.

Mark schemes

These are similar to those an examiner would use to complete the initial marking of a script. Each scheme highlights the points that will score marks. However, they are for guidance and do not necessarily illustrate the only correct interpretation. Some answers may be different and equally valid and would therefore be awarded equal marks. The mark schemes will help you focus your attention on what the examiner is looking for in the award of marks. Do not be tempted to read these mark schemes before you attempt to answer the questions. Use the examination papers as if they were the real thing.

Sample answers and examiner comments

After each examination paper, there is a script that reflects the type of answer required for the award of a grade A. This answer is not perfect, but is sufficient to achieve 80% or more. Throughout the sample answer, examiner comments are preceded by the icon *e*. These comments reflect the strengths and weaknesses of the answer. A final heading goes through a list of potential errors and omissions commonly associated with the question.

Extract 1 Regulating European labour markets: more costs than benefits?
J. Addison and S. Herbert, *IEA Hobart Paper 138*. (Reproduced by permission of the Institute of Economic Affairs.)

Extract 2 The euro: explanatory notes
European Commission Europaper. (Reproduced with the kind permission of the European Commission, Directorate-General for Economic and Financial Affairs, 200 Rue de la Loi, B-1049 Brussels, Belgium. The copyright of the contributors is hereby acknowledged: ©CECA-CEE-CEEA, Bruxelles–Luxembourg, 1998.)

Extract 3 The transition economies
Economic Review Data Supplement, Vol. 16, No. 1.

Extract 4 Central and East Europe
Barclays Economic Review. © *Barclays Economic Review*, Fourth Quarter 2000.

Extract 1

Regulating European labour markets: more costs than benefits?

Institute of Economic Affairs (1999)

(1) The present British government has signed on to the social chapter, the provisions of which are now an integral part of the European Union treaties.

(2) European Union social policy can be traced back at least to 1974, even though the treaty basis for social legislation is very narrow.

(3) The extension of majority voting under the 1986 Single European Act made it easier to pass social legislation. After the 'social charter' was proclaimed in 1989, legislative proposals 'came thick and fast', some making 'creative use' of health and safety criteria.

(4) The 1997 Treaty of Amsterdam not only contains the provisions of the earlier Agreement on Social Policy but includes an employment chapter which 'opens up scope for considerable Commission activism in the future' and is a 'central plank of social policy'.

(5) Market failure arguments may provide a basis for political intervention in the labour market but they are not clear cut. Furthermore, it is difficult to specify mandates which will deal adequately with market failures, and government corrective action will itself be subject to failure.

(6) Britain and other countries with less regulated labour markets have been better at creating employment opportunities than the more regulated major EU states.

(7) Empirical studies generally show that the net effect of employment protection and similar rules is 'lower employment, greater and longer unemployment for some and, implicitly, a decline in the speed with which labour relocates from declining to growing sectors of the economy'.

(8) Not all employment regulations will have the same effect. But the 'upward harmonisation sought by the Commission' has potentially serious costs in terms of 'disemployment and reduced employment growth'.

(9) The Commission has failed to meet its obligation to evaluate the possible effects of its social proposals on the labour market. Its efforts have been amateurish and have taken place in an 'analytical vacuum'.

(10) Its proposals should in future be subject to independent efficiency audit, not to prevent the development of social policy but to provide information on the employment and other consequences of new mandates.

To conclude: in evaluating mandates the following issues have to be addressed. First, one has to identify, in the manner of Table 1, the sources of market failure that the policies are designed to correct. Table 1 summarises the possible market failure arguments that could be deployed to defend the main EU directives. The difficulties associated with these arguments have to be squarely confronted.

Table 1 Mandates and market failure

Directive	Possible market failure justification	Explanation
Training	Externalities	Firms might 'poach' trained workers.
Health and safety	Misinformation, monopsony, externalities	Workers might be unaware of hazards — partly because safety information is a public good — and also perhaps be forced into dangerous work due to lack of mobility etc.
Collective redundancies	Misinformation, externalities	Prior notice might enable workers to search better. Might also be second best benefits.
Written contracts	Misinformation, monopsony	Workers might be unaware of contract terms, and also perhaps be forced to accept unfair terms due to lack of mobility.
Child labour	Misinformation, myopia	Young workers and their parents might be poorly informed about the benefits of education (a type of merit goods argument).
Posted workers	'Destructive' competition (negative externalities across countries)	If posted workers do not receive host country wages and conditions, this bids down wages and conditions.
Pregnant workers	Asymmetric information	Fear of adverse selection might prevent firms setting up maternity leave schemes.
Working hours	Monopsony, misinformation/myopia	Lack of choice might force workers to work overlong hours. Workers might not know what is good for them.
Atypical workers	'Destructive' competition	Some countries encourage atypical work, which might give them an unfair advantage.
European works councils	Asymmetric information	Fear of adverse selection might prevent firms setting up co-determination schemes; there might also be externalities from 'traditional' firms.

Second, one has further to specify the parameters of individual mandates. Third, one has to move from theory (and specification) to policy. It cannot be presumed that the government can be relied upon to correct matters. Only if the cost of market failure outweighs the cost of potential government failure is the mandate indicated on efficiency grounds.

The principal source of government failure — apart from self-seeking behaviour on the part of the bureaucracy and politicians — is informational, for reasons associated with the diverse nature of markets and market participants. This latter consideration assumes even greater importance in a pan-European setting given the diversity of the constituent market economies. Here, the need to examine the specifics of the market failure argument is most clearly underlined: since market failures will differ between countries, this can only undermine the case on welfare grounds for harmonisation.

Efficiency is not the only justification for mandates. There is also the question of equity. Indeed, equity appears by default to be the principal basis for Commission activity in the area of social policy. Two major issues are posed here. First, among those in work, the disadvantaged appear more likely to be harmed than helped by mandates placing floors under working conditions. This prediction follows logically because mandates will disrupt mainly low-wage labour markets. Second, measures that may notionally increase earnings equality may not do the same for incomes in the presence of disemployment effects. Here the fundamental question is whether the focus should be upon employment mandates that benefit only those in employment. It is all too easy, therefore, to envisage mandates that are the worst of both worlds, serving to increase both inefficiency and inequality.

Extract 2

The euro: explanatory notes

European Commission (1998)

The advantages for the consumer fall into two main categories: the specific benefits of a direct nature, and the (often more important) benefits linked indirectly to the introduction of the euro.

(1) The first of these are clearly perceptible. They consist primarily of:

- The disappearance of foreign exchange commissions in the case of journeys to one of the partner countries in the euro zone (the classical example of a person travelling with 1,000 francs in his wallet to the 14 other member states and changing his money in each will currently return with less than 500 francs without even making any purchases).
- The ability to transfer funds very cheaply and very easily to other countries in the euro zone.
- Price transparency — it will be possible to compare prices in different member countries directly. This will strengthen competition and cause prices to fall.
- The disappearance of exchange risks.

(2) The creation of the euro has important indirect effects as well. These are:

- a better functioning of the single market
- a low level of interest rates and the associated stronger growth of investment
- greater currency stability
- low inflation thanks to the stability-oriented monetary policy conducted by the European Central Bank

All these advantages will have a positive effect on growth.

Extract 3

The transition economies

Economic Review Data Supplement (1998)

The transition economies of the former Soviet Union and Eastern Europe have faced an enormous task in attempting to introduce market reforms and move away from central planning. Table 1 contains some key data about some of these countries, together with data about the UK and Greece to provide some framework for comparison (the UK because you know something about it, and Greece because it is the lowest-income member of the European Union).

Figure 1 shows GDP per capita for 1995, measured in international (PPP) dollars. These measurements, which are produced by the United Nations Development Programme, are preferred to those using US dollars because they are a more accurate reflection of the purchasing power of local income. To help put these data into perspective, you might be interested to know that Moldova has GDP per capita of a comparable level with that of Nicaragua or Côte d'Ivoire — just a little above Uganda or Bangladesh.

Figure 1 GDP in the transition economies, 1995

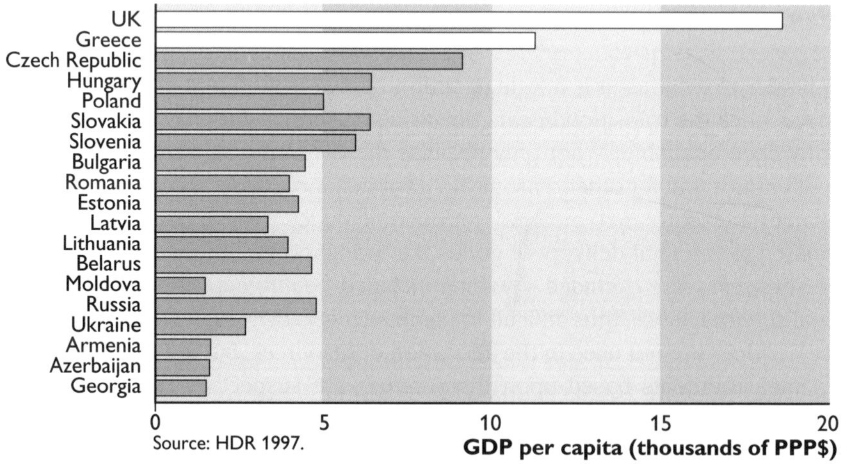

Source: HDR 1997.

Table 1 Key data on the transition economies

	Female life expectancy at birth		Registered unemploy-ment rate	Net foreign direct investment % of GDP	Internet users (/100,000 people)	Tertiary students (/100,000 people)	% of labour force in agriculture	Inflation (% p.a.)
	1990	1995	1995	1993	1994	1992	1990	1985–95
UK	–	79.3	8.7	–1.1	228.4	2405	2	5.1
Greece	–	80.4	–	1.3	21.1	1907	23	15.4
Slovenia	77.3	76.8	13.9	–	50.2	2033	6	–
Czech Republic	76.0	76.9	3.0	3.9	61.9	1132	11	12.2
Hungary	73.7	74.5	11.1	6.5	46.0	1145	15	19.9
Slovakia	75.4	76.3	13.8	1.3	14.6	1247	12	10.6
Poland	75.5	76.4	14.9	2.0	16.5	1527	27	91.8
Russia	74.3	69.7	2.8	0.1	0.7	3174	14	148.9
Belarus	75.6	75.2	2.7	0.1	(.)	3317	20	–
Bulgaria	75.4	–	11.4	0.5	0.9	2085	13	45.9
Estonia	73.1	73.1	1.8	3.8	49.8	2603	14	77.2
Romania	75.2	74.9	8.9	0.3	1.4	1019	24	68.7
Lithuania	76.2	73.1	6.1	1.2	1.8	2802	18	–
Latvia	74.6	74.3	6.4	0.8	13.0	2786	16	72.4
Ukraine	75.0	71.7	0.4	(.)	0.6	3152	20	–
Armenia	75.2	72.7	6.9	–	0.3	3711	18	183.1
Azerbaijan	74.8	75.9	1.0	1.2	(.)	2323	31	–
Georgia	76.1	73.5	3.1	0.2	–	2710	26	310.0
Moldova	71.8	74.3	1.4	0.3	(.)	2665	33	–

Sources: TransMONEE, HDR 1997, WDR 1997.

Note: Countries are in descending order of GDP per capita; the UK and Greece are included for comparative purposes.

For a number of reasons, it is a little difficult to judge the extent to which income levels have changed since the transition began. This is because GDP data for these countries have only recently been available — not only because the countries themselves did not exist as independent entities, but for other reasons also. For instance, under a communist regime, the GDP-equivalent measure (net material product) includes only physical production and services related to the final delivery of goods (i.e. transport etc.). However, so-called 'non-productive services' were excluded — which included health, education, defence, banking and personal services. It was thus difficult to compare levels of living with the capitalist world. In any case, if prices are not used in the allocation of resources, but are artificially set by the state, then measurements based upon those prices are suspect as expressions of value. Stories have circulated, suggesting that prices had been set at such distorted levels that many East German steel plants had been producing negative value-added until they were drawn into market-based production in a reunified Germany — in other words, the value of output was less than the value of the inputs used in production. This had been hidden by the distorted prices imposed by the state.

Another factor to bear in mind in this connection is the size of the 'hidden' economy. In all countries, the value of GDP per head is probably understated as a result of transactions which are not recorded. However, it seems clear that the size of these hidden transactions is especially large in the case of the transition economies. Indeed, in the case of Russia, it is estimated that transactions in the black economy exceed the value of those that are reflected in the official GDP measurements! In Poland, it is estimated at around 45%, as compared with just 12% in Britain and 6% in Switzerland (as reported in the *Guardian*, 3 January 1998).

A particular problem of making the transition is in enabling prices to find their appropriate market levels when they have been centrally controlled for a period of time. In many of the transition economies, this has resulted in high levels of inflation. You can see this in Table 1 for many of those countries where data are available. Such high levels of inflation are likely to be damaging in a number of ways, not least in making it difficult to encourage firms to undertake investment.

Another interesting feature revealed by Table 1 is the fact that the agricultural sector remains important in many of these countries, contributing a large share of GDP in 1990. A large agricultural sector is one common characteristic of many developing countries. This raises the question of whether many of these 'new' countries on the international scene should be regarded as being part of the developing world, especially given the relatively low levels of GDP per head that we identified above.

There are some key differences. On the one hand, these economies in transition face some very different sorts of problems in adapting to allowing markets to guide resource allocation. On the other hand, it is apparent that levels of health and education are rather higher than in the developing countries of Africa or south Asia. This is shown in the data relating to life expectancy (which tells us something about the health levels of the population) or the number of tertiary students (which says something about education).

Education is especially significant in the process of economic development. Other things being equal, we would expect a country beginning with relatively low levels of income to be able to expand more rapidly than one that had high income levels. This is known as the convergence hypothesis, which argues that late-developing countries should be able to learn from the experience of early developers and thus grow more rapidly. This hypothesis does not seem to have been effective for the developing countries, which have remained trapped at low levels of development (with only a few exceptions, mainly in east Asia). However, one argument that has been put forward to explain this is that the developing countries do not have sufficient levels of human capital to enable them to take advantage of the technology developed in the industrial countries. It is here that the transition economies may gain. In spite of having income levels that are comparable to those of many developing countries, the transition economies have generally better standards of education and health, and may thus be in a better position to gain from technology transfer.

Some evidence on the extent to which this is likely to happen may be seen in the data provided on foreign direct investment, where in some cases (Hungary, the Czech Republic and Estonia) there have clearly been quite substantial flows of funds heading into these countries.

The number of internet users relative to population suggests that technology is not yet as widespread as it is in the West.

Figure 2 shows the pattern of net migration in some of these countries. The size of these flows is startling in some instances. Notice around half a million people migrating into the Russian Federation. The civil strife that has accompanied the transition in some of these countries has no doubt added to the migration figures.

Figure 2 Net migration in selected transition economies

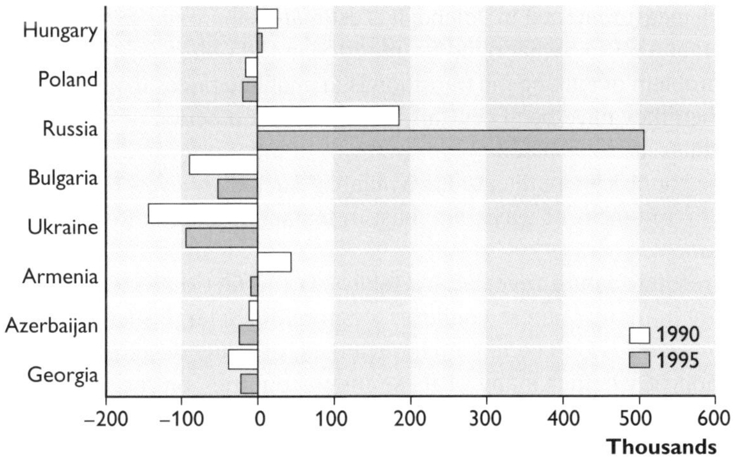

Not shown in the data is the quality of the environment, and the prevalence of poverty in many of the transition economies. These are serious problems that will need to be addressed as steps are taken towards development and, perhaps, eventual integration into the European market.

Extract 4

Central and East Europe

Barclays Economic Review (Fourth Quarter 2000)

The **Russian** economy is recovering well, with real GDP growth of 7.4% year-on-year in the first half of 2000 and 5.5% forecast for the full year. The recovery largely reflects higher prices for energy exports, improved competitiveness in the tradable goods sector and a recovery in gross fixed investment. In **Poland**, growth is expected to remain buoyant this year but delays associated with the 2001 budget could compound political problems, potentially resulting in early parliamentary elections. Real GDP in Hungary is forecast to rise by 5.5% this year, underpinned by strong export growth. The current account deficit is forecast to narrow to 3.6% of GDP, due, in particular, to improvements in the balance on services. **Bulgaria** continues to recover strongly from the adverse consequences of last year's Balkan conflict, with real GDP growth of 5.2% in the first half of the year, more than double the rate recorded in the same period last year. Second-quarter growth in the **Czech Republic** slowed sharply to 1.9% year-on-year from 4.4% in the first quarter. Rising domestic demand and buoyant investment underpinned the second-quarter growth, replacing the export-led recovery of the first quarter. Although **Romania** remains conspicuous as one of the region's biggest laggards, 1% growth is forecast this year, ending three successive years of recession. Meanwhile, a poor agricultural harvest will combine with high world energy prices to widen the current account deficit to a forecast $1.9 billion.

Table 1 Key Central and East Europe forecasts

	1999	2000	2001
Growth (%)			
Bulgaria	2.4	4.5	4.5
Czech Republic	–0.2	2.5	3.0
Hungary	4.5	5.5	5.5
Poland	4.1	5.0	5.0
Romania	–3.2	1.0	2.5
Russia	3.2	5.5	3.5
Current account ($bn)			
Bulgaria	–0.7	–0.6	–0.6
Czech Republic	–1.1	–1.4	–1.9
Hungary	–2.1	–1.8	–2.7
Poland	–11.7	–12.0	–12.1
Romania	–1.3	–1.9	–1.8
Russia	25.0	40.4	30.6

Figure 1 Growth: annual percentage changes in real GDP, Central and Eastern Europe and the world, 1980–2000

Turkey recovers

Although **Turkish** output contracted sharply in 1999, a new economic programme supported by the IMF and the World Bank provided some encouragement. So far this year, real GDP has rebounded sharply, with first-half growth of 5.7% year-on-year, as consumer credit and fixed investment have responded to sharp falls in interest rates. However, high energy prices and a crawling peg exchange rate regime have combined to widen the current account deficit precipitously to a forecast $8.5 billion for this year.

Figure 2 Turkey: growth (%) and current account ($bn), 1990–2001

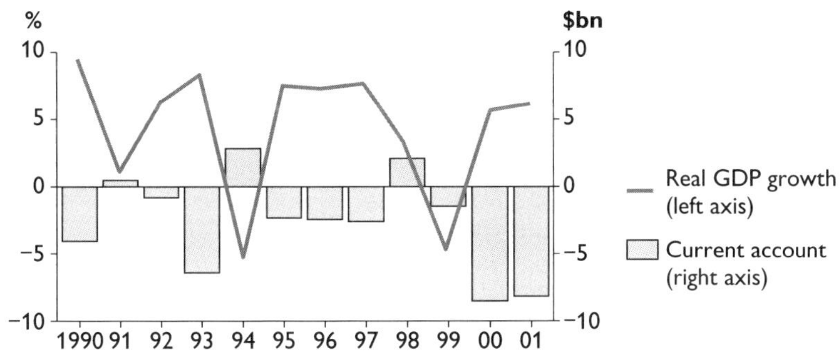

Extract 1 The Common Agricultural Policy in the balance
S. Rickard, *Economic Review*, Vol. 17, No. 1.

Extract 2 Feasibility and likelihood of a free-market agriculture
R. Johnson and R. Howarth, from 'Reforming the EU farm policy: lessons from New Zealand', *Institute of Economic Affairs Occasional Paper 112*. (Reproduced by permission of the Institute of Economic Affairs.)

Extract 3 Monetary policy in the euro area
From a speech by W. Duisenberg, 25 January 1999. (Reproduced by permission of the European Central Bank.)

Extract 4 Monetary policy in the United Kingdom
Bank of England fact sheet. (Reproduced by permission of the Bank of England.)

Extract 5 The euro: better late than never?
J. Hearn, Institute of Financial Services. (Reproduced by permission of J. Hearn, Institute of Financial Services/CIB.)

Extract 6 The euro: explanatory notes
European Commission *Europaper*. (Reproduced with the kind permission of the European Commission, Directorate-General for Economic and Financial Affairs, 200 Rue de la Loi, B-1049 Brussels, Belgium. The copyright of the contributors is hereby acknowledged: ©CECA-CEE-CEEA, Bruxelles–Luxembourg, 1998.)

Extract 7 One side of the coin
J. Forder, *Economic Review*, Vol. 17, No. 3.

Extract 1

The Common Agricultural Policy in the balance

Economic Review (September 1999)

The CAP's founding fathers adopted the policy of open-ended price support to achieve their main objective. The idea is very simple. In order to increase the production of, say, wheat, cereal farmers will be guaranteed a minimum price of, say, £100 per tonne, no matter how much they produce. This removes some of the uncertainty associated with agricultural production and provides farmers with the near certainty that revenue will exceed costs. The principle can be demonstrated using the neoclassical model of the firm operating under perfect competition, as shown in Figure 1.

For simplicity, let us assume the farm grows only wheat. Given a fixed area of land, the farm's production will be subject to the law of diminishing returns: the farmer will face the normal U-shaped average and marginal cost curves as shown. In the absence of the CAP, the farmer faces the market-generated price, P_m, and might reasonably plan his business so that, on average, a normal profit is expected (point A): this is achieved by planning to produce output Q_0.

Figure 1 Price and individual farm output

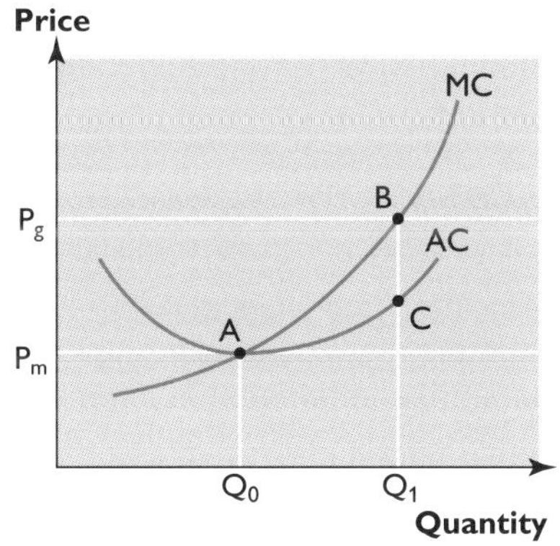

If now the authorities guarantee a higher price, say P_g, the farmer will plan to increase production to Q_1. The need for a guaranteed price is clear: to achieve this higher output the farmer must use more fertiliser and increase the use of labour and machines to spread the fertiliser and harvest the crop. This is represented by the rising marginal cost curve. But despite the rising costs, with price P_g the farmer now has the incentive of supernormal profits — on a unit basis represented by the vertical distance BC — if output is increased.

The level of the guaranteed price is a political decision. Originally, the CAP set guaranteed prices at a level designed to generate an income sufficient to support a family working a small farm. This was deliberate, as the founding fathers had wider objectives than just producing more food. In particular, they had a social objective. They wanted to arrest the population drift from rural to urban areas. This was partly driven by the fear of unemployment in urban areas and partly by the desire to maintain an economically viable rural economy. However, as we shall see, it was the muddling of production and social objectives that caused many of the CAP's problems.

Extract 2

Feasibility and likelihood of a free-market agriculture

Institute of Economic Affairs (2000)

> It had its place to cushion the massive migration from agriculture to industry. It may have served to balance French and German economic interests. I have yet to see why a CAP is indispensable today. (Dahrendorf 1979, quoted in Hallett 1981)

It seems clear that the CAP has become a blundering dinosaur whose extinction is long overdue — a triumph of political expediency over economic logic. Indeed, *The Economist* (1990) described it as 'the single most idiotic system of economic mismanagement that the rich western countries have ever devised.' And even the Commission itself (EC 1987) has been forced to concede that: 'It does therefore seem doubtful whether farmers in fact benefit from support.' The conclusion must be that agriculture in the EU should be returned to a free market.

Lessons from New Zealand

For a long time the proponents of support argued that a free market would lead to the ruination of farming and its associated industries and social distress in rural communities. Johnson's paper chronicling the New Zealand experience shows that the reality is otherwise. Farm policy reform was part of a general move to deregulate the economy and cut public expenditure. The effects of a rapid transition to a free market were nowhere as severe as had been predicted, although it took about 7 years for the reforms to work through product, factor and labour markets.

Farm incomes fell in the short run, but not severely; there was no wholesale movement out of rural areas — in dairy, sheep and fruit farming employment fell by only 12% between 1986 and 1991 — not much more than the normal trend; the prevailing structure of family farming continued; export earnings have been maintained; land values inevitably fell, but for many these were only paper losses, and have recovered again as new markets have been found and farm incomes have risen again; the trend of amalgamations and increasing farm size has been somewhat accelerated; welfare assistance was required but only in the short term and less extensively than had been anticipated. The extent to which farmers were satisfied with the reforms is attested by the visits made by leaders of the New Zealand farmers' unions in the early 1990s to Britain and the Continent when they extolled to farmers' meetings the virtues of the free market and exhorted European farmers also to take the plunge into a bracing cold shower which would rid them of the constant uncertainty of government meddling and control.

Specific proposals for the CAP and for Britain

The Treaty of Rome (1957) states that: 'The common market shall extend to agriculture and trade in agricultural products.' It is proposed that this (free internal agricultural trade) plus free external agricultural trade should be the only common agricultural policy of the EU. Recognising the political impossibility of ever reaching agreement on a free-market agriculture throughout the 15 countries, farm policy should come under the 'subsidiarity' provisions of the EU, which are already agreed in principle — that national governments should be left to control those areas which are best managed at national level — and repatriated. Repatriation is already the stated policy for fisheries of the British Conservative Party. In order to put the administrative framework into place, it would have to be staged over, say, 3 years.

Thereafter, national governments would be free to spend as much or as little as they liked on their farmers, *provided the spending was not linked to production and did not distort internal or international agricultural trade.* EU-wide policies on environmental protection would not be precluded. Direct income support (not linked to a product) to provide a modest base income for farmers in areas of difficult and beautiful terrain ('less-favoured areas') to ensure the continuation of farming in them on social and aesthetic grounds; special pension schemes for older farmers; retraining grants for younger farmers; and transitional payments to ease the pain of change over a limited period of, say, 5 years would be permissible. No doubt individual governments would vary in their generosity with their taxpayers' money in providing such programmes according to the political clout of their agricultural interests. Schemes such as the present arable area payments and set-aside which enable intensive production to continue on the remaining acreage and are mainly of benefit to larger farmers would not be allowed. Although any form of income support might be argued to keep production at a higher level than the free market would dictate, the modest amount allowed above would have an insignificant effect on overall output.

A free-market agriculture would be perfectly feasible for British farmers and it would return to British consumers the freedom of choice to purchase their food from the most efficient sources all over the globe. But it could not be introduced overnight, given the present level of support under the CAP, which is about twice as high as that in New Zealand in 1984 before their reforms. The shocks to factor and land markets and the rural economy would be too severe. After repatriation, a pre-announced gradual let-down over, say, 5 years would be best. A temporary compensation payment to ease the transition might be paid to all 'professional' farmers (not to 'hobby' farmers or those for whom farming was not the main source of household income) as prices were reduced. It could be either a once-and-for-all lump sum or a decreasing annual payment to avoid an abrupt cut-off. For simplicity it could be paid per acre or per livestock unit or per ton of product in a base period.

Extract 3

Monetary policy in the euro area

Extracts from a speech made by the President of the European Central Bank, Dr Willem F. Duisenberg (25 January 1999)

The Treaty on European Union, commonly referred to as the 'Maastricht Treaty', assigns the European System of Central Banks (ESCB) the primary objective of maintaining price stability in the euro area. Price stability is to be maintained over the medium term. According to the Governing Council's published definition, price stability has been defined as a year-on-year increase in the Harmonised Index of Consumer Prices (HICP) for the euro area of below 2%. Neither would deflation — that is, a persistent fall in the price level — be consistent with price stability. The annual rate of inflation in the most recent available data of around 1%, measured on this harmonised basis, is consistent with the definition of price stability.

Monetary policy needs a forward-looking, medium-term orientation. This takes into account the fact that monetary policy affects the price level only with variable, usually long and unpredictable time lags. It is not able to control all short-term movements in the price level.

The stability-oriented monetary policy strategy rests on two 'pillars'. The first pillar is a prominent role for money. This is deemed to be important on account of the essentially monetary origins of inflation over the longer term. The second pillar of the monetary policy strategy is a broadly based assessment of the outlook for price developments and the risks to price stability in the euro area as a whole. The Governing Council recognises that it is important, in parallel with the assessment of monetary growth, to look at a wide range of financial and other economic indicators, including economic forecasts.

The Governing Council does not react mechanistically to a single variable — whether this be a forecast, the exchange rate, unit labour costs or fiscal indicators — but rather takes into account the complete picture offered by all available and meaningful leading indicators of future inflation. In this context, the Governing Council analyses the economic reasons behind the projected risks to price stability. The appropriate monetary policy response to a threat to price stability will depend on the nature of the threat.

Monetary developments can reveal useful information about future price developments and thereby offer an important compass for the conduct of monetary policy. Consequently, the Governing Council of the ECB has announced a quantitative reference value for broad monetary growth as measured by M3, which should, under normal circumstances, give some indication of future inflationary pressure. The choice of M3 as an aggregate is supported by empirical evidence regarding the long-run stability and leading indicator properties of this aggregate. Moreover, conceptual arguments pointed to the considerable importance of including in the monetary aggregate those assets which have a high degree of substitutability with narrower definitions of money. Therefore, in addition to currency in circulation and deposits, repos, units or shares of money market funds and money market paper as well as short-term debt securities, all of which are close substitutes for more traditional bank deposits, have also been included in this definition.

The first reference value for M3 growth has been set at an annual rate of 4.5%. This reference value is consistent with the maintenance of price stability over the medium term, while allowing for sustainable output growth and the trend decline in the velocity of circulation of M3. In setting the reference value for monetary growth, the Governing Council has taken account of various factors and emphasised its medium-term orientation. First, the Governing Council is committed to maintaining price stability according to the definition enshrined in the Treaty on European Union. This requires increases in the HICP for the euro area of 'below 2%'. Second, the Governing Council takes the view that a figure in the range of 2% to 2.5% per annum for the trend growth in real GDP in the euro area appears to be reasonable. Third, the uncertainties concerning short-term developments in velocity linked to the start of Stage Three have led the Governing Council to assume that the medium-term trend decline in velocity lies approximately within a range of 0.5% to 1% each year. This range reflects historical experience over the past 20 years.

Substantial or prolonged deviations of current monetary growth from the reference value should, under normal circumstances, signal risks to price stability in the medium term. Monetary policy does not react to deviations of monetary growth from the reference value in a 'mechanistic' way. In the first instance, such deviations will be thoroughly analysed to infer any signals which they may offer about the prospects for price developments. If the deviation points to a threat to price stability, monetary policy will react in a manner appropriate to counter this threat, rather than attempt to eliminate the deviation of monetary growth from the reference value in the short term.

Its performance in maintaining price stability in the medium term should be used by the public to judge the success of the Eurosystem.

The Eurosystem's monetary policy stance is not one of benign neglect with respect to the exchange rate. The Eurosystem's stability-oriented monetary policy strategy takes into account the external value of the euro as one, potentially important, determinant of the outlook for price stability. Obviously, if a strong and abrupt appreciation of the euro were to occur, this would lead, all other things being equal, to downward pressures on price developments. In such a situation, there would be a stronger reason for lowering the ECB's interest rates, which might then, in turn, help to counteract part of the prior exchange rate movement.

However, monetary policy reactions to the exchange rate, or to any other variable, can never be mechanistic or automatic. According to its stability-oriented strategy, the Eurosystem always has to analyse carefully a wide set of indicators, the nature of any disturbances and their implications for the overall outlook for price developments in the medium term. In any case, it must be borne in mind that the Treaty on European Union also requires the single exchange rate policy to respect the primary objective of price stability. Thus, the ECB cannot commit itself in advance to any specific reaction with respect to the exchange rate.

I am sure you would agree with me that it would not necessarily be appropriate to tighten the monetary policy stance simply because the euro had depreciated, if, at the same time, we were in a recession with increasing downward pressures on prices. As such mechanistic reactions to exchange rate developments could easily endanger price stability and destabilise economic developments in the euro area, we deliberately excluded any kind of exchange rate targets or target zones from our strategy.

The Eurosystem is open, transparent and, above all, accountable for its performance. As part of its communication strategy, the Governing Council of the ECB regularly informs the public about changes in its assessment of the monetary, economic and financial situation in the euro area and about specific monetary policy decisions. The Governing Council meets every fortnight. The first meeting in every month is immediately followed by a press conference and the release of the President's Introductory Statement, which is a summary of the conclusions of the Governing Council with regard to its assessment of monetary, financial and other economic developments. This is similar to what other central banks call minutes. We are convinced that this very prompt delivery of information serves the interests of the public in an optimal way. I do not think that many central banks publish their minutes only a few hours after the meeting of their governing body. I am also convinced that it is in the public interest for the view of the whole Governing Council to be presented, rather than the views of individual members. Moreover, the ECB has just published its first edition of the Monthly Bulletin, and will publish an Annual Report. We shall also explain our policies on a regular basis in speeches and interviews, also making a presentation to the European Parliament at least four times a year.

Extract 4

Monetary policy in the United Kingdom

Bank of England fact sheet (1999)

The current framework for monetary policy is provided by the 1998 Bank of England Act, which formally gives the operational responsibility for setting interest rates to the Bank of England. Under these arrangements, the Bank's monetary policy objective is to deliver price stability (as defined by the Government's inflation target) and, subject to that objective, to support the Government's economic policy, including its objectives for growth and employment. The Government's inflation target will be confirmed in each Budget Statement. In June 1997, the Chancellor announced that he was setting the Bank a target of 2.5% for retail price inflation excluding mortgage interest payments (RPIX).

Decisions on interest rates are normally made by the Monetary Policy Committee (MPC) of the Bank which was established by the 1998 Bank of England Act. The MPC consists of the Governor and the two Deputy Governors of the Bank, two members appointed by the Bank after consultation with the Chancellor, and four members appointed by the Chancellor. A representative of the Treasury attends meetings in a non-voting capacity.

The MPC meets monthly. Decisions are announced immediately after the meeting and the minutes are published 2 weeks later (though there are provisions for delaying publication of information on market intervention by the MPC in certain circumstances). Increased accountability to Parliament and the public is achieved through the publication of the minutes, and the continued publication of the Bank's Inflation Report, as well as through appearances by MPC members before the Treasury Select Committee of Parliament and through the Bank's Annual Report. The Governor is also obliged to write an open letter to the Chancellor if inflation deviates more than 1% on either side of the 2.5% target. Under certain circumstances, the Bank of England Act allows the Treasury to give instructions to the Bank in the field of monetary policy for a limited period of time. These powers can only be used if the Treasury is satisfied that they are required in the public interest and only by 'extreme economic circumstances'.

Operations in the domestic money market

The main instrument of monetary policy is the short-term interest rate (see Box 1). Central banks have a variety of techniques for influencing interest rates but they are all designed, in one way or another, to affect the cost of money to the banking system. In general this is done by keeping the banking system short of money and then lending the banks the money they need at an interest rate which the central bank decides. In this country such influence is exercised through the Bank of England's daily operations in the money markets.

The Bank of England is banker to the UK banking system. Transactions between commercial banks are finally settled between accounts held at the Bank of England by banks — 22 at present — which are members of the wholesale clearing systems. These settlement banks are expected to hold positive balances on their accounts at the Bank each day. The commercial banks' total funds are altered by transactions between themselves and the Bank, and between themselves and the Government accounts at the Bank. Transactions between banks merely redistribute funds between themselves. Payments from the private sector to the government are finally settled by a transfer of funds between the settlement banks' accounts at the Bank and the Government's accounts. Thus, by managing the money flows the Bank can affect the size of the settlement banks' balances with itself.

Box 1 The effects of interest rates

A change in interest rates will affect the economy through a number of routes. First, a change in the cost of borrowing will affect spending decisions. Interest rates affect the relative attraction of spending today as against spending later, as a rise in rates will make savings more attractive and borrowing less so, and this will tend to reduce present spending, both on consumption and on investment.

Second, a change in rates affects the cash flow of borrowers and creditors. A rise or fall in interest rates affects the cash flow of those with floating interest rate assets or liabilities. For example, many households have floating interest rate deposits in banks and building societies. Floating interest rate debtors include households with mortgages, and companies. Fluctuations in cash flow may affect spending.

Third, a change in interest rates affects the value of certain assets, notably housing and stocks and shares. Such a change in wealth may influence people's willingness to spend.

Fourth, a particular pressure on prices comes through the exchange rate. For example, a rise in domestic interest rates relative to those overseas will tend to result in a net inflow of capital and an appreciation of the exchange rate. A rising pound will reduce prices for imports, thus increasing competitive pressures and supplementing the downward pressure on inflation arising from weakened demand.

All of these influences on demand are likely to affect prices and inflation. A rise in short-term interest rates can be expected to restrain demand for UK output in the way described. That in turn is likely to put downward pressure on UK prices and the rate of inflation.

Extract 5

The euro: better late or never?

Institute of Financial Services (1999)

Forget the emotion, the issue is quite simple: do we join a monetary system that will forever fix the value of sterling to the value of a broader monetary aggregate which covers the countries of the European Union? Let us start by looking at the anticipated advantages and disadvantages of such an action.

In favour

A report from the EU commission stated that the efficiency gain from removing currency uncertainty and exchange rate costs may be worth as much as 10% of the gross national product. Many academics have considered this to be an overestimate but agree that there are cost advantages to anyone trading in Europe, including individuals who may be taking a holiday in Europe. Changing currency is time-consuming and costly.

A single currency will remove an artificial restriction to free trade within Europe. Arguably greater trade freedom brings about a more efficient allocation of resources where the most efficient firms prosper and grow while the least efficient wither and disappear. For farmers, this process will remove the 'Green Rate' which creates price differences when none should exist.

The euro will create more price stability in individual countries by removing any opportunity to speculate on the price movement of a currency. There are a lot of speculative funds sloshing around the world, looking for opportunities to make a quick gain on currency differentials. Short-term speculation based upon little more than rumour can change the value of a currency even though there has been no change in economic fundamentals.

People who trade throughout Europe will be certain of the price they agree under contract for a future delivery. Before the euro, a firm would have to bear the risk of an unexpected currency change which could turn a profit-making situation into a loss overnight.

The analysis of monetarist economists who have analysed monetary stability throughout Europe since 1945 shows the UK lagging behind the other main players in Europe, particularly Germany. It is argued that, particularly during the 1970s, the Bank of England had a poor record on inflation and therefore it will be an advantage to join a European Central Bank where individual members have a much better track record on monetary stability.

The anticipated monetary restrictions that will be applied by the ECB will act as a discipline on the government fiscal policy. This will stop politicians overspending, particularly in the run-up to a new election.

Against

At the other extreme, there are academics who estimate that the cost advantages of a single European country are negligible or less than 0.1% of GNP. At the same time, they point out that there will be significant costs involved in the transition to a single currency (compare with decimalisation).

Price stability is not guaranteed under a single currency. It will depend upon the type of policy adopted by the ECB. This institution will be run by a cartel, and history has shown that, when decisions are made by a group of people with different political agendas and target numbers, it is likely that agreement will lean towards the larger number rather than the smaller number. It is therefore probable that a country acting alone will be able to achieve a lower target.

Because economies are dynamic there is support for flexibility in exchange and interest rate policy. Arguably, adjustments to these variables can solve certain problems by affecting everyone a little bit rather than a few people a lot if unemployment results. As soon as the UK interest rates are a thing of the past it is possible that employment levels will be the factor that will adjust to economic changes in individual countries. An American economist, Anna Schwartz, wrote of the euro:

> A grandiose conception is to be imposed on over 300 million inhabitants of 15 countries, who speak 11 different languages, are subject to different political and legal institutions and live in economies that vary in their performance. The question that promoters of monetary union have not answered is whether the barriers to economic growth that confront these economies boil down to the absence of a single central bank and a single currency.

The UK will no longer be able to use its fiscal policy to manage the overall level of economic activity in the economy. Keynesians particularly would not want to lose the opportunity to fine-tune economic variables by changing the balance between government income and expenditure.

An often forgotten problem is at what rate do we fix sterling irrevocably to the euro? Arguably, the current price of sterling against the euro is distorted by interest rate differentials between the UK and the EU. There is a 3% difference in nominal rates which is slightly reduced for the real rate of interest. On several occasions in the past the UK has entered a European monetary union. The last time we entered, interest rates were high and the current account of the balance of payments was negative. These are both factors which signal an overvalued currency and, on this and previous occasions, the UK seemed to benefit from falling out. However, once in, you cannot fall out of a single-currency agreement.

It has not been the purpose of this article to persuade you one way or the other, but rather to place in front of you some of the advantages and disadvantages so that, when it comes to it, you can make a more informed decision.

Extract 6

The euro: explanatory notes

European Commission (1998)

A single currency for the single market

EMU is the culmination of the single market and will enable consumers and economies to take full advantage of the benefit of competition and of a better international division of labour.

A single market with a single currency will permit more transparency, more competition and a better division of labour.

More transparency:

Importers, exporters and investors must be able to make an accurate calculation of the cost of their activities and the return on them. Lack of transparency and the possibility of unexpected currency movements compel them to include a risk premium in their cost calculations. This restricts movements across borders, in particular for small and medium enterprises, which are the least well-equipped when it comes to managing the exchange risk.

More competition means:

- Preventing the formation of monopolies and other collusive practices, which limit growth prospects by an inefficient allocation of production factors.
- Compelling industrialists to incorporate technological progress into both their production process (efficiency of production, rationalisation and productivity gains) and their products (improvement in quality). What is true of technical progress is also true of innovations in the field of management and commercial practice.

Moreover, EMU will allow the consumer to obtain the best product at the lowest price.

A more efficient division of labour makes it possible to:

- Ensure that each individual specialises in the area where he enjoys the greatest comparative advantage (the division of labour therefore makes first and foremost for greater efficiency).
- Generate additional income which can be divided between the trading partners. Specialisation creates wealth in that it permits a gain in both quantity and quality. Since the Second World War, international economic development has stemmed directly from the systematic and unprecedented scale of exploitation of this reserve of growth.

Europe has succeeded in achieving a high degree of economic integration.
The liberalisation of trade is a historical phenomenon which goes back a long way and is not confined to the European Union. However, never before has any regional grouping made up of sovereign entities succeeded in taking economic integration as far as the European Union has done:

- Customs duties between European countries started to come down steadily in the early 1950s and disappeared entirely in 1968 with the introduction of a simple customs union and the implementation of the common external tariff.
- The official proclamation of the single market on 1 January 1993 marked the ending of non-tariff barriers to trade between member states.
- The internal market is almost complete. The opening-up of public procurement has recently been achieved, and that of services is under way. The sectors which are still compartmentalised are few.
- The liberalisation of capital movements and the abolishment of exchange controls have improved the allocation of capital at the European level, from which the peripheral economies have been the first to benefit since they are now able to finance their development more easily.

EMU will make it possible to complete European economic integration by guaranteeing the establishment of sound and transparent competition.
The disappearance of the national currencies will mean that the prices of goods can be directly compared on the markets of the participating member states, which will now merge into one. This does away with transaction costs and the exchange risk — two obstacles to trade.

The competitive positions of companies can no longer be overturned by exchange rate movements but will reflect productivity, inflation and cost differentials. This greater transparency should permit a better allocation of capital and of available resources. The greater transparency of conditions of competition should also facilitate the international comparison of balance sheets, the transparency of export prices, mergers, acquisitions and alliances at Union level and, more generally, company development strategies.

Over and above its positive effects on price stability and public finances, the single currency will make it possible to complete the single market and increase the benefits which have already flowed from it.

Extract 7

One side of the coin

Economic Review (February 2000)

Benefits: transactions costs and uncertainty

The basic point in favour of a single currency is that it reduces transactions costs in trade and travel, and eliminates uncertainty about future exchange rates. These are both supply-side benefits. The first releases the factors of production involved in currency transactions for employment in a genuinely productive activity. The second promotes the efficient allocation of international investment. For many people, this is the whole story about the economics of a single currency, and it makes it hard to see how there could be any objection which is not from some other realm, such as politics.

Costs: economic policy autonomy

The basic cost, however, is in the loss of economic policy autonomy. This is something different from the political idea of sovereignty, which is about the *right* to control one's policy. Autonomy is about the *ability* to control it. In a single currency area, there cannot be different interest rates in different places. This is fundamentally because of the opportunity for arbitrage. Hypothetically, if there were different interest rates in France and Germany, borrowers in the high-interest country would seek to borrow in the low-interest one, whilst lenders were doing the opposite, and the two interest rates would converge. This might also happen with separate currencies, of course, but in that case there is the extra consideration of exchange rate changes. A British borrower who borrows at currently very low euro interest rates in euroland incurs the risk that when the time comes to repay, the euro will have risen and the debt will be much bigger. For this reason, such international transactions are limited and interest rates do not equalise. But members of a single currency lose their ability, not just their right, to set interest rates.

How important is the loss of this ability? That is a question about which there can be much argument. If one part of a monetary union is booming, and another is in recession, the booming area would benefit from higher interest rates whilst the recession area needs lower ones. Bad policy for somebody would seem to be inevitable. The inability to set appropriate interest rates is the basic cost of a single currency. This suggests that the appropriate cost–benefit analysis for Britain is a comparison of the likely future costs of having the same interest rate as the rest of Europe with the benefits of exchange-rate certainty and lower transactions costs.

The opponents of the single currency will point to the present condition of the British economy as an example of the benefits of national autonomy. Interest rates on the Continent are low, and perhaps set to fall further, because of concern over high levels of unemployment. In Britain, unemployment is much lower, and if continental interest rates applied here, the consequence would presumably be inflation. In my book *Both Sides of the Coin* I identified several other similar cases in present-day and recent European experience which seem to show the benefits of different policies.

Counter-argument: fiscal freedom and national divides

On the other hand, the advocates of British membership have two thought-provoking arguments. One is that whilst monetary policy, in the form of interest rates, cannot be used autonomously in a monetary union, there is more room for fiscal policy independence. So, for example, any British boom threatened by lower interest rates in monetary union could be controlled by higher British taxes.

Secondly, there is the point that the problem in question already arises within existing countries. In Britain, the recent tendency for the southeast of England to experience much greater inflationary pressure than the north is a perfect example. In fact, Christopher Huhne produces data in his half of *Both Sides of the Coin* that suggest that such different developments *within* existing countries in the European Union are as large and frequent as those *between* countries. This, he argues, suggests that if one thinks this is a serious problem with the euro, it must also be that existing countries are too large to have single currencies. And yet, one does not hear serious suggestions that the United Kingdom should have several separate currencies.

Conclusion

So, I believe there are two dangers in EMU. One is that inappropriate policy will have to be set for some countries some of the time because all countries must have the same interest rate. The other is that in adverse circumstances, should they arise again, policy will be set single-mindedly to control inflation, and the consequence will be rising unemployment. The fact that government's use of fiscal policy in recessions is also subject to limitation — albeit somewhat flexible — cannot improve this situation, but it can make it worse.

The problem for Britain, of course, is that so much of the rest of the EU has committed itself to the euro. In my view, that is a great mistake, and an unfortunate one for Britain since we cannot be helped by a European disaster. But on the other hand, better policymaking in Britain can partly insulate us, and it gains us nothing to make the same mistake as others.

Extract 1

Russia

Barclays Russia Report (December 1999)

Summary

- Economic mismanagement, allegations of corruption and the misuse of constitutional power have irrevocably weakened President Boris Yeltsin's authority. Political activity is focused on the December parliamentary elections and, more importantly, on the 3 June 2000 presidential elections.
- In the parliamentary elections, the Communist Party is expected to lose seats, while parties of the centre are likely to gain considerable support. The outcome of the presidential elections is far from clear, but prime minister Vladimir Putin is a strong candidate. Alternatively, a more nationalist candidate could be elected.
- The highly unstable situation in the North Caucasus — with regions seeking independence on ethnic grounds — highlights the weakened political authority of the federal government in relation to Russia's federal territorial units.
- Russia is now experiencing a degree of economic stability following the August 1998 economic crisis. The economy is forecast to grow slightly this year, due to recovery in industrial production (although from a low base). Relatively tight monetary policy and relative exchange rate stability has helped slow inflation. Continuing weak domestic demand is likely to delay any sustainable economic recovery until at least after the presidential elections. Considerable structural problems remain, not least the restructuring of the banking sector.

- Although the fiscal position has improved, with revenues up due to recovery in production and increases in energy prices, debt servicing obligations have not been met fully, while the budget figures ignore the continuing problem of arrears and costs associated with the Chechen conflict.
- Relations with the IMF are likely to remain difficult (loans are currently being withheld), with the Russian government clearly distracted by the Chechen crisis and the upcoming elections rather than progress on reform and policy implementation. Further interruptions to the release of IMF credits can be expected.
- Severe international liquidity problems remain, with the government failing to make scheduled foreign debt service payments requiring on-going official and commercial foreign debt restructuring. Despite a sharply improved current account surplus, international reserves remain very low. The low level of reserves reflects the government's limited ability to access export revenues, minimal foreign direct investment (FDI) and a pick-up in capital flight — which is likely to increase further in the run-up to the presidential elections.

Table 1 Key economic indicators

		Average 1993–97	1996	1997	1998(e)	Forecasts 1999	2000
Real GDP growth (%)		–6.1	–6.0	0.8	–4.6	1.0	1.5
Consumer prices (%)		288.3	47.6	14.6	27.8	90.0	33.0
Budget balance/GDP (%)		–7.3	–7.9	–7.0	–5.0	–3.0	–3.0
Trade balance ($bn)		17.7	23.1	17.4	17.4	29.0	24.3
Current account balance ($bn)		7.6	12.1	4.1	2.5	18.3	16.8
Current account balance/GDP (%)		2.4	2.8	0.9	0.9	8.9	7.7
International reserves (excl. gold) ($bn)		9.7	11.3	13.0	7.8	7.0	7.0
Import cover (months)		2.6	2.7	2.8	2.3	2.6	2.3
Foreign debt ($bn)		128.3	125.2	162.6	169.8	166.5	168.5
Debt service/exports (%)		5.0	6.5	6.4	13.4	19.0	19.4
Exchange rate:	Rouble/$ (average)	3.7	5.1	5.8	9.7	25.0	32.0
	Rouble/£ (average)	5.8	8.0	9.5	16.1	40.5	51.2

Recent trends and outlook

Domestic economy stabilises

According to preliminary figures, real GDP was 0.8% higher year-on-year in the first three-quarters of 1999, compared with the corresponding period of last year (measurement of GDP, though, remains notoriously difficult). The recovery from a very low base in the third quarter largely reflects increased industrial production, up some 7% year-on-year over the same period. Recovery has been strongest in construction, chemicals, metallurgy, coal, machinery, and wood and paper products and indicates a strong import-substitution effect due to the sharp devaluation of the rouble. Consumption and investment demand remain weak, suggesting that further strong growth in industrial production in 2000 will be limited.

Although doubts remain about the reliability of official figures, weak real GDP growth is forecast for this year, revised up from negative growth mainly due to the strong recovery in industrial output. Sustainable economic recovery will be delayed until real household incomes — which are sharply down — recover and there is strong investment growth (the latter is likely to be put off until after the presidential elections).

Lower inflation

The combination of relatively tight monetary policy and relative exchange rate stability has helped slow monthly inflation to 1.4% in October (57.1% year-on-year), compared with almost 12% in December last year (84.6% year-on-year). Producer prices, however, have generally been increasing faster than consumer prices, particularly in industry and construction (the producer price index was up 5.5% in October), aggravated in part by the pick-up in oil prices.

Even if the authorities are able to avoid a sharp renewal of exchange rate pressures, monthly inflation is forecast to edge up slightly early next year as some relaxation of fiscal policy is anticipated in the run-up to the presidential elections and producer prices feed through to consumer prices.

Figure 1 Real GDP growth and inflation, annual percentage changes

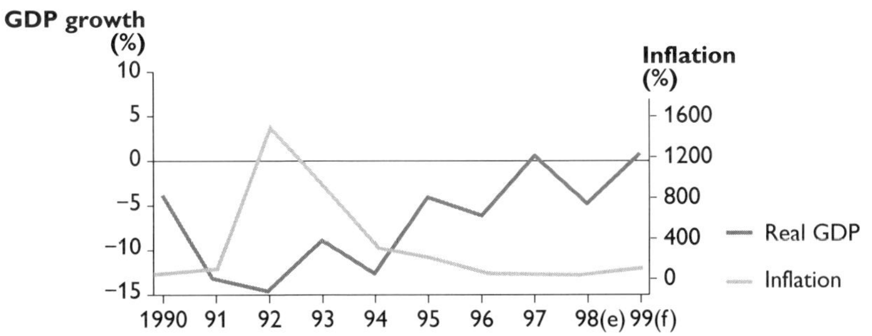

Improving current account...but precarious international liquidity

The international liquidity position remains very fragile and is likely to remain unstable. Despite a sharply improved current account surplus, the government has failed to make scheduled debt service payments and international reserves remain very low. At the end of October, foreign currency reserves were only $7.1bn (excluding gold), compared with $7.8bn at the end of last year. The low level of reserves reflects the government's limited ability to access export revenues, minimal foreign direct investment (FDI) (some $2bn in 1998) and a pick-up in capital flight (estimated at some $2.0–3.0bn per month) — which is likely to increase still further in the run-up to the presidential elections. Moreover, there may be further interruptions to the release of IMF credits over the next year.

Figure 2 Trade and current account balance, $bn, 1990–1999

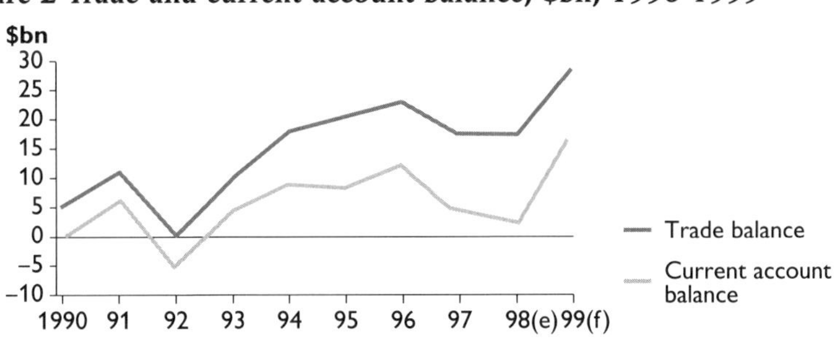

Economic policy

Improving fragile fiscal position

The shortfall in the budget deficit for January–September was RUB62.7bn, estimated at some 3.5% of GDP, compared with a deficit of 4.4% of GDP over the corresponding period of last year. Interest payments on debt amounted to RUB117.5bn (of which RUB53.6bn was interest on domestic debt), or about a quarter of total expenditure. This equates to a primary budget surplus (excluding interest payments) of RUB54.8bn or some 3% of GDP over the period, as against a target for the year as a whole of 2.0% (in aggregate, no primary surplus was achieved last year). Total revenues have improved largely due to a stronger than expected recovery in production and in commodity prices. Increases in energy prices are significant, with revenues from oil and gas accounting for about a third of budget revenues. On the expenditure side, the improvement reflects the fact that public sector wages are down sharply in real terms, while debt servicing obligations have not been met fully. The favourable budget figures also ignore the continuing problem of public sector wage and pension arrears, while it is unclear about the costs associated with the Chechen conflict. Based on the available information, the overall fiscal deficit is forecast at 3% of GDP this year.

The Duma approved the 2000 federal budget in early December in the fourth and final reading. Approval in the upper house Federation Council is required before it is placed before the president for final acceptance as law (further amendments to the budget are not anticipated). The planned primary surplus is 3% of GDP. The planned rise in the primary surplus in 2000 partly reflects increases in export tariffs on crude oil and oil products and the planned introduction of a 5% export tax on natural gas. The 2000 budget also assumes foreign debt service of about $5.0bn and foreign credits of some $5.9bn.

Russia has a long way to go before it achieves a sustainable fiscal policy. A number of factors continue to limit tax collection: the under-reporting of economic activity, the low 'monetisation' of the economy (resulting in barter trade), a lack of payments discipline, the general ineffectiveness of tax administration and poor regional tax policy. Successful fiscal reform hinges on an appropriate institutional and legal framework that cannot be developed quickly. The almost complete lack of a tax culture implies continuing fiscal problems.

Monetary policy

Monetary policy remains relatively tight, with rouble broad money (M2) rising 31.8% in the first 8 months of the year, which has helped slow monthly inflation. The central bank is due shortly to issue short-term rouble-denominated debt — the first tradable domestic bonds since the government defaulted on domestic debt last year — giving the bank a powerful tool to regulate the money market and aid budget deficit financing. Following a fall in the rouble/US dollar exchange rate of over 70% in nominal terms in the last 6 months of 1998, the rouble has since been rather stable. This has been underpinned by administrative and liquidity restrictions by the central bank. At present, dollar supply tends to exceed demand because of the requirement that exporters should sell up to 75% of their revenues on the domestic currency market, while dollar demand has weakened due to the collapse of imports. The central bank is expected to continue to support the currency in a managed float, with next year's budget forecasting an annual average exchange rate of RUB32/$.

Table 2 Key monetary indicators

		1995	1996	1997	1998(e)	1999(f)
Consumer prices (% change)		197.4	47.6	14.6	27.8	90.0
Money supply (M2) (% change)		112.6	29.6	28.0	37.5	NA
Deposit rate (%)		102.0	55.1	16.8	17.1	14.0
Lending rate (%)		320.3	146.8	32.0	41.8	40.0
Stock market index		132.0	359.4	811.7	355.2	NA
Exchange rate:	Rouble/$ (average)	4.6	5.1	5.8	9.7	25.0
	Rouble/£ (average)	7.2	8.0	9.5	16.1	40.5

Figure 3 Exchange rates: monthly averages, 1994–2000

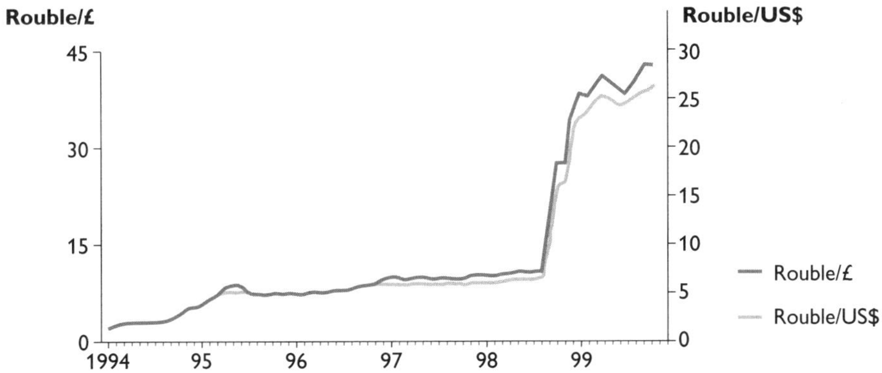

Extract 2

International trade

European Commission (1998)

Spillover effects from the economic performance in the EU

Economic and monetary union will result in an amplification of the type of economic benefits that followed from the 1992 programme. The following major categories of permanent effects are expected to result from the creation of EMU:

- Microeconomic efficiency gains, arising from the elimination of exchange rate uncertainty and transaction costs within the Union, thereby stimulating trade within the EU and thus leading to a permanent increase in output. While these effects can be expected to raise the level of output and real income on a permanent basis because of a higher overall factor productivity and a larger capital stock, growth would be increased during the transition to this higher-growth steady-state.

- Macroeconomic stability effects, arising both from the elimination of intra-EU exchange rates and from greater discipline in monetary and fiscal policies, which will lower the risk premia built into interest rates and thus lead to higher investment. These stability effects will also reduce the variability of output, prices and other macroeconomic variables. As such variability permanently reduces the level of output through its impact on uncertainty, a reduction of variability will also benefit economic growth. In this respect, also, the risk of long-term exchange rate misalignments should be mentioned: these give rise to a misallocation of resources and may even lead to protectionist pressures, thus posing a threat to free trade. Given the high level of economic integration in the EU, these effects may be particularly harmful, and even threaten the well-functioning of the single market.

The European Commission (1990) estimated that the transaction costs related with the existence of different currencies in the EU amounted to around 0.5% of GDP in the mid-1980s. An IFO study quoted in European Commission (1996) estimated these costs at almost 1% of GDP on average over the period 1986–1995. The efficiency costs related to resource misallocation are more difficult to evaluate, as the extent to which risk premia would decline is hard to ascertain, but they may be even larger. Baldwin (1990) estimated that a reduction in risk premia of 0.5 percentage points could lead to an increase in EU GDP by between 5% and 10% in the long run. Also the impact on economic growth of other effects resulting from the creation of EMU is difficult to quantify. However, there is broad agreement that the introduction of the euro will give a substantial growth impetus to the countries of the EU, as output and real income move to a higher-level steady-state.

As a result, the EU demand for imports from non-EU countries will also be boosted. The size of this effect of course depends critically on the share of the EU as a market for a third country's exports. Also, exporters from non-EU countries will be able to exploit the benefits of EMU, as regards the complementation of the single market, just like European companies. As argued in European Commission (1996), the creation of the single market has led to external liberalisation towards non-EU countries, because market access has been made easier with a single system, and this effect will be reinforced by the introduction of the euro.

While the effect of the introduction of the euro on growth in Europe is difficult to quantify, a number of simulation exercises have been presented by the IMF. In IMF (1996), earlier simulations of convergence scenarios were updated for the period 1996–2000. These scenarios focus on the impact of the convergence programmes of the member states (the macroeconomic stability effects) and in particular on the impact of the reduction of general government deficits. These adjustment measures produce short-run losses in output relative to the baseline scenario, but average GDP growth for the period 1996–2000 is higher than in the baseline, in which no fiscal adjustment measures are taken. In a scenario in which all countries are assumed to make the necessary fiscal adjustment to achieve a 3% deficit in 1997, acquiring credibility in the process, GDP growth is 0.9 percentage points higher than in the baseline scenario towards the end of the period. IMF (1997) presents a scenario in which EMU serves as a catalyst for further structural reform. On the fiscal side, an additional reduction of government spending of 2% of GDP is assumed over the medium term, and on the structural side, it is assumed that product market liberalisation, reinforced by the efficiency gains from the introduction of the euro, will lead to a rise in total factor productivity, while labour market reform will lead to greater real wage flexibility and a reduction in the natural rate of unemployment. In this scenario, the level of output in EMU member countries lies almost 3% higher than in the baseline scenario in the medium term (2010). By 2002, GDP exceeds that of the baseline scenario, reaching 1%. IMF (1997) presents also the impact on GDP growth in non-EU countries (see Table 1).

Table 1 Impact of EMU on economic growth (percent deviations from baseline scenario)

	2000	2001	2002	2003	2010
EMU members	0.2	0.9	1.0	1.1	2.9
Non-European G-7	–0.1	0.0	0.0	0.1	0.1
Other industrial countries	–0.1	0.1	0.1	0.0	0.2
Developing countries	0.0	0.1	0.2	0.2	0.3

Source: International Monetary Fund

It appears from these simulations that even if the effect on the member countries of the euro area may be substantial, the impact on non-EU countries may be relatively small on average. However, the aggregation used in these IMF simulations masks developments in individual countries or regional groupings of countries which will be affected much more by higher growth in the EU than it would appear from Table 1, e.g. because of their close trade and economic links with the countries of the EU. This will in particular be the case for the countries of Central and Eastern Europe, the Mediterranean countries, and certain countries in Africa which will be linked to the euro area through their exchange rate (the countries that are currently members of the CFA franc zone).

Spillover effects from the higher synchronisation of business cycles in the EU

As a result of the functioning of the single market and the impact of financial integration, business cycles have tended to become more synchronised within the EU, and this phenomenon is expected to continue with the completion of EMU. As a result, cyclical fluctuations within the euro area will increasingly affect other regions in the world, through trade relations, the coupling of international financial markets, and fluctuations in the exchange rate of the euro.

The European Commission (1997c) analyses the role of EMU in business cycle behaviour in the member states participating in the euro area. The authors discuss various business cycle models, and conclude that in all models the adoption of a common currency in a particular region would, to some extent, lead to a greater synchronisation of business cycles in that region. A number of empirical studies are reviewed, and it is concluded that already at the present stage cyclical output movements in the European Union are broadly synchronous. This result is attributed to two factors: first, the higher degree of interdependence of the economies of the EU countries which is the result of the expansion of international trade and of international capital flows among the member states, and second, the closer policy convergence, mainly during the last decade.

The European Commission (1997c) also looks at the relationship between the exchange rate regime and the business cycle, but finds only very limited empirical evidence for the existence of such a relationship, given that the cyclical characteristics of most macroeconomic variables, with the exception of the real exchange rate, in general do not depend on the exchange rate regime. Nevertheless, the authors conclude that the introduction of the euro will further increase the degree of synchronisation of economic cycles in the participating member states. This will be the consequence of three main factors: increasing trade interdependence, increasing financial market integration, and increasing convergence of economic policies.

In the euro area, the likelihood of country-specific policy shocks will be minimised as a result of the existence of a single monetary policy and coordinated fiscal policies constrained by the Stability and Growth Pact. To the extent that economic shocks will become more symmetrical, and consumption smoothing and investment financing through international borrowing and lending will become even more important after the introduction of the euro, cyclical fluctuations will further converge.

Given the higher degree of synchronisation of business cycles within the euro area, cyclical fluctuations within the euro area will increasingly affect other regions in the world, through trade relations, the coupling of international financial markets, and fluctuations in the exchange rate of the euro. The impact of a higher degree of synchronisation of economic cycles in the euro area on non-EU countries is hard to quantify; moreover, it will vary from one country to another, depending on the degree of economic interdependence of the country with the EU. The only conclusion that can be drawn at this stage is that economic developments in the EU will increasingly make themselves felt in the economies of non-EU countries.

The impact of the introduction of the euro on non-EU countries will depend crucially on the share of these countries' trade with the countries of the euro area in their total external trade, and on the trade elasticity of these countries' economic growth.

Extract 3

The euro: explanatory notes (1)

European Commission (1998)

Economic and monetary union — a key factor in sustained growth and stability

The introduction of the euro on 1 January 1999 will help overcome the main obstacles which have curbed economic growth over the last 20 years:

- currency disturbances
- a conflict between budgetary policy and the stability objective assigned to monetary policy

Currency disturbances within Europe have been costly in growth and employment terms over the last few years. The turmoil in the spring of 1995 played a major role in the cyclical slowdown starting in the second half of 1995. The overall impact can be estimated at a loss of approximately 2 percentage points of growth and 1.5 million jobs over the 1995–96 period.

Exchange rate risk will be eliminated within the euro-area. Intra-European trade accounts for a considerable proportion of member states' total trade (between 49% and 75% according to the country in question). Furthermore, the euro will provide Europe with better protection against fluctuations in the dollar, given that the euro is expected to become a major transaction currency, enabling a significant proportion of European exports to be invoiced in euros.

The fall in interest rates which the euro will bring about is linked to three factors:

- control of government debt, the servicing of which alone currently corresponds to 40% of household saving and is at the expense of private borrowers
- the elimination of risk premiums on long-term interest rates linked to inflation expectations and exchange rate risk
- the size of euro securities markets, the liquidity of which will attract new financial investors

A 'crowding-in' effect on private investment will thus be witnessed: better economic prospects and interest rates, leading to more investment, more growth, higher tax revenues and lower government deficits, will complete the virtuous circle by leading again to lower interest rates.

These direct effects will be matched by renewed confidence on the part of industrial and financial investors, the impact of which could be considerable.

Extract 4

The euro: explanatory notes (2)

European Commission

Does budgetary consolidation promote growth and employment?

The argument that budgetary consolidation would be deflationary is contradicted by economic developments in Europe and the United States over the last 20 years.

Budgetary consolidation is a necessity with or without monetary union, for two main reasons:

- Excessive public deficits inevitably lead to a crowding-out process as a result of the high levels of interest rates that they engender and the associated drain on national savings. Consequently, they hold back any increase in growth potential and thus impede job creation.
- The accumulation of public debt ultimately renders the burden of debt servicing intolerable. This snowball effect deprives the public authorities of any margin of manoeuvre. This burden is a constraint on the forms of expenditure that are properly the responsibility of the state, notably infrastructure investment, the financing of education and research, and social spending.

In the medium term, budgetary consolidation presents a number of advantages:

- it redirects saving to investment, which benefits from better rates of interest

- it allows the state to reorganise its revenue and expenditure in a more efficient manner and recreates some margin of manoeuvre in budgetary policy
- the reduction in the public deficit gives rise to expectations of a decline in the tax burden which itself generates a decline in precautionary saving

It is expedient to undertake a reorganisation of the public finances as far as possible during an economic upswing. However, a decision not to pursue a budgetary consolidation process that has become indispensable on account of unduly sluggish growth may give rise to a risk of even weaker growth, not to mention recession. Any delay may be severely penalised by the financial markets, resulting in higher risk premiums on interest rates and in fresh strains on foreign exchange markets. A sound process of budgetary consolidation is one that is announced, credible, socially balanced and complied with.

Even in the short term, budgetary consolidation has positive effects:

- In the heavily indebted countries that face a substantial risk premium on their interest rates, the announcement and implementation of a credible budgetary consolidation programme may bring about a rapid and marked decline in those premiums. Such a decline reinforces the budgetary consolidation process by reducing debt servicing.
- Even leaving aside the risk-premium effect, a reduction in the public deficit has beneficial effects on interest rates, in both the long and the short term, thereby encouraging domestic demand investment and consumption.
- Last but not least, private investment may be very quickly substituted for public consumption, offsetting the fall in demand mechanically induced by the budgetary consolidation process. This crowding-in effect will be all the more rapid if the return on investment is high, as is the case in Europe at the moment. Alongside a short-term demand effect, the increase in the rate of investment creates new capacity and enhances the medium-term growth potential, which is of crucial importance in the fight against unemployment.

Paper 1

Time allowed: 1 hour 45 minutes

A copy of the pre-issued case study is included with the question paper. All your answers should be in continuous prose; they will be assessed on the quality of the written language.

Total marks allocated: 60.

(1) Extract 1 addresses market failure in European labour markets.

(i) Explain and illustrate how a competitive labour market determines wages. (5 marks)

(ii) Table 1 refers to a number of mandates which are aimed at overcoming possible market failures. With reference to 'Health and safety', explain the potential failures that the directive is addressing. (5 marks)

(iii) Assess the potential impact on low-wage labour markets of the implementation of European mandates and say whether there is likely to be any difference between short-term and longer-term effects. (5 marks)

(2) Extract 2 explains a number of advantages to the consumer of his or her country being part of the euro zone. Explain what is meant by the euro zone and identify the advantages that may benefit producers in this zone. (20 marks)

(3) Extracts 3 and 4 make reference to the 'transition economies' of Europe.

(i) Explain what is meant by the process of transition and comment upon why it has been undertaken. (10 marks)

(ii) To what extent can the current living standards in transition economies be compared with those that existed under central planning. (15 marks)

Mark scheme

(1) (i) Expect a brief explanation of the downward-sloping demand curve and the upward-sloping supply curve in a labour market and the equilibrium wage rate (3). It will not be necessary to explain the demand curve using marginal revenue productivity theory to achieve full marks, although students who have studied Module 2884: 'Economics of Work and Leisure' may include it. A clearly labelled diagram is required for the remaining marks (2).

(ii) Full marks can be achieved from an explanation of 'misinformation, monopsony and externalities', although a candidate can also achieve full marks by reference to any relevant market failures (5).

(iii) An explanation of how the implementation of European mandates will raise costs in low-wage labour markets. In the short term, this may cause unemployment and disadvantages in competition with other producers outside the European Union who do not comply with similar standards. In the longer term, there will be benefits to the employee that may manifest themselves in improved productivity, motivation etc. (5).

(2) The euro zone consists of those 12 countries within the European Union that participate in economic and monetary union (EMU) (3). This question asks the student to focus on the benefits to the producer, much of which can be deduced from the explanation of the consumer advantages of being part of the euro zone. These advantages may include:

- the removal of foreign currency transaction costs
- more efficient transfer of capital
- price transparency throughout the euro zone for products and productive factors
- removal of exchange-rate risk
- clearly identifiable borrowing and saving rates
- consistent monetary policy aimed at stable and low interest rates and stable prices with low inflation
- overall improvement in efficiency, productivity and economic growth
- single large market with potential for economies of scale

(17 marks)

(3) (i) An explanation of the changeover from command economies that were under central direction of resources to market economies that allow the price mechanism to allocate resources (4). In order to explain why it has happened, it will be necessary to focus on the inefficiencies of command economies and the potential benefits of a market economy. The explanation is likely to be supported by comparative evidence from western and eastern Europe (6).

(ii) Comparisons can be based upon GDP per capita and purchasing-power estimates as well as deduced from other statistics, such as life expectancy, investment, literacy, etc. However, problems are caused where:

- countries did not originally exist, e.g. Slovenia
- inflation has distorted real figures
- measures of GDP did not include services
- administered prices did not reflect market prices
- value of output was less than the value of inputs to production
- there was a black market or hidden economy
- quality of the environment is/was poor
- there has been a change in leisure hours
- unproductive capital goods (armaments) have been replaced by consumer products
- there were changes in political stability

(15 marks)

Response to paper 1: grade A answer

(1) (i) In a competitive labour market, it is assumed that profit-maximising employers are competing with each other to hire labour, while employees are competing with each other for jobs. The market is illustrated below.

The demand for labour is derived from the demand for the product and the slope of the curve is determined by the marginal revenue product of labour. As the wage rate rises, so more workers will be attracted to this market. However, the same rise will cause a reduction in the demand for labour as the costs of production rise and profits can only be maximised by employing fewer people. At wage rate W_1 the quantity of labour demanded by the producer will equal the quantity of labour Q_1 which is willing to supply itself for work.

5/5 marks

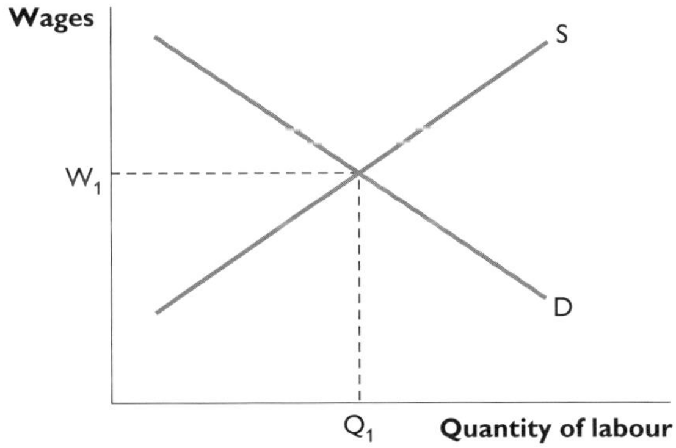

A good answer which includes all the information required and a clearly labelled diagram. The theory is explained in Module 2881: ' The Market System' under the specification heading 'Competitive markets and how they work'.

(ii) Table 1 refers to external costs to society of the labour market not functioning efficiently because of a variety of health and safety issues. An external cost is not paid for at the point of production but it nevertheless imposes a cost upon society. Two potential causes of external costs are identified. Firstly, misinformation: this occurs when the employer and/or the employee are unaware of potential hazards that may exist in the production of a particular product. The result may be that society is damaged when people are injured or even killed while they are at work. The explanation in Table 1 refers to safety information as a public good. A public good is non-rival and non-excludable. This means that producers do not have incentives to search for safety information because, once the information is available, people are not excluded from the knowledge and therefore no one will be willing to pay for the information. A question arises as to whether the employer is legally responsible for the safety of the employee and, if this is the case, then the potential to prosecute does actually internalise this problem and the external cost no longer exists.

A second point is referred to as 'monopsony'. A monopsonist in the labour market is the sole buyer of labour and it is suggested that, because the employee has no alternative employer, he or she will be forced to accept the terms of employment of the monopsonist. The profit-maximising employer will seek to minimise costs and maximise revenues and this may mean ignoring the costs involved in installing all the necessary safety procedures. Arguably, this same scenario will exist with many competitive firms whose existence will depend upon them achieving the lower costs of production.

5/5 marks

This is a very good answer. Not only does it expand upon the issues highlighted in Table 1, but it also questions the validity of the points set out to justify potential market failure.

(iii) Superimposing the European mandates on competitive markets for products and the productive factor labour will raise the costs of producing products. This will shift the supply curve for the product to the left and create a new equilibrium for the product at P_2Q_2. The reduction in demand for the product will reduce the demand for labour at each and every wage rate and shift the demand curve for labour to the left, as illustrated in the diagrams below:

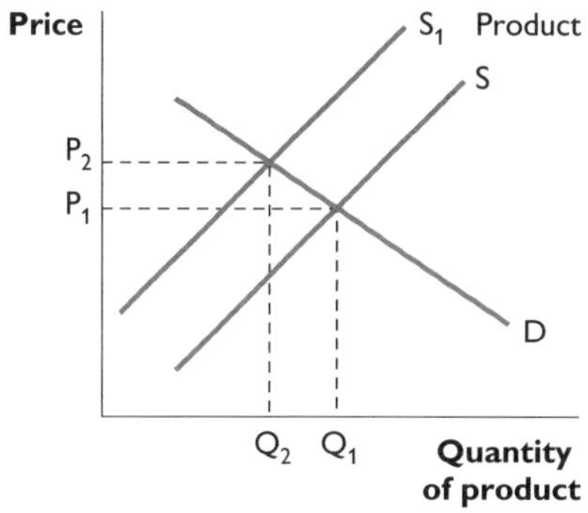

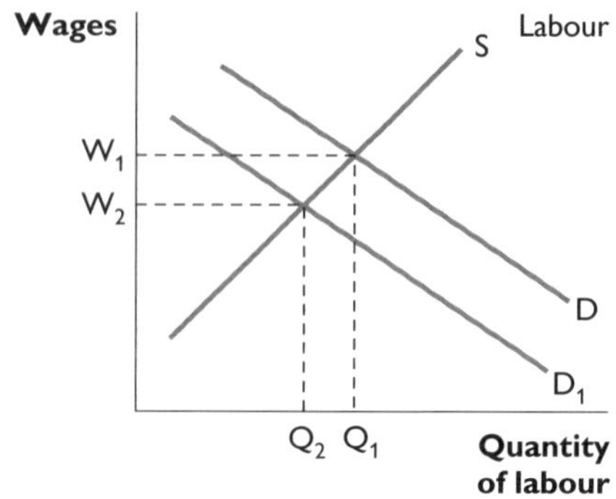

The wage rate will fall from W_1 to W_2 and the number of people employed will contract from Q_1 to Q_2. In the short term, the impact of the higher costs may be particularly damaging in industries competing with firms located outside the European Union which are not subject to the same cost increases.

However, over the longer term, the labour markets and associated firms and industries may benefit from greater safety and health. It may improve labour productivity as fewer working days are lost and workers feel safer and more motivated in their jobs. Also, if working hours are reduced then employees will not be suffering from stress and overwork and this may help to improve efficiency.
4/5 marks

A good answer that deals with the likely short-term and long-term effects of the potential higher costs of implementing the European mandates. However, 1 mark is lost because the student does not emphasise the fact that the potential damage will be more acute where wages are already low. Here, wages may fall even further or unemployment rise even higher if minimum wages are already in place.

(2) The euro zone refers to the 12 countries of the European Union which have fully adopted the strategy set out for economic and monetary union (EMU). In January 1999 (January 2001 in the case of Greece), they all fixed their currencies irrevocably to the euro at an agreed rate. There is no flexibility for currencies to move in value against the euro, and although national currencies will remain in circulation until 2002, this year has been agreed as the one when the euro will finally replace domestic currencies. After that year, all trade in each country in the euro zone will be in the single European currency. The UK, Denmark and Sweden have not adopted the euro, despite being members of the European Union.

Producers in the euro zone will benefit from not having to trade currencies before they trade products. This will reduce transaction costs and remove exchange rate risk. In business there is usually a delay between orders, deliveries and final payments and, during that time, the value of a currency may change — to the detriment of the business if the currency has depreciated.

The prices of products and productive factors throughout the euro zone will be transparent and this will speed up decisions and avoid confusion. The international firm trading throughout Europe will find that transferring funds and accounting for costs and revenues will be significantly more efficient. Also, the ease with which price comparisons can be made will strengthen competition.

As well as a single currency, the euro zone has a monetary policy in place which aims to ensure monetary stability, currency stability, price stability and low interest rates. Low interest rates will encourage firms to expand output by investing in more capital up to the point where the marginal efficiency of capital is equal to the interest rate. This and a low rate of inflation are now considered to be the most important factors in promoting economic growth. Another advantage of low interest rates is that consumers will be encouraged to borrow more and this will boost the aggregate demand for goods and services and encourage firms to expand output in a more profitable environment.

A final advantage to firms in the euro zone is the overall size of the single market. Some firms will be able to expand in order to take advantage of the economies of scale that may be available in certain industries.
17/20 marks

e The explanation of the euro zone achieves full marks and, overall, the answer deserves maximum marks for quality of language. However, slightly more detail could have been expected in a 35-minute answer.

(3) (i) The process of transition in Europe refers to the break-up of the USSR and its satellite countries, which were governed as command economies, into independent countries that adopted markets and the price mechanism as a way of allocating resources. Originally, the command economies had approached the problem of scarcity through total planning. There were no private property rights and income was received from work rather than ownership. Production and productive factors were under the direction of a central authority and quotas were usually established for productive units. Where markets existed, prices were usually fixed and shortages and surpluses were used to signal an expansion or contraction of output.

The system described above was difficult to manage, resources were inefficiently allocated and improvements in living standards were slow. It was difficult to hide the facts of improving living standards in western Europe from the people of eastern Europe, and gradually there was a growing demand for political and economic freedom and a dismantling of the huge bureaucracy that had been required to manage the command economies. People of the transition economies hoped that freedom of contract, private property rights, consumer sovereignty and market forces would harness self-interest and, in the pursuit of profit, bring about the economic growth that would fulfil consumer expectations for higher living standards.

8/10 marks

(ii) There is a range of statistics available to compare living standards over time in the same country. The most commonly used is gross domestic product per capita, although the United Nations has developed the Human Development Index for such comparison.

Before and after the transition process had begun, GDP figures could be used for comparison. They would need to be adjusted for any changes in population size to produce per capita figures. Also, comparisons would be made difficult where countries did not exist before the break-up of the USSR and the separation in Czechoslovakia and in Yugoslavia.

Over the requisite period, inflation has both accelerated and decelerated to such an extent that nominal figures would be useless in comparison. Therefore, a deflator would be required to produce real (output) figures. When the USSR was a command economy, its measures of GDP included only tangible goods, and therefore that component of output that included services was not recorded.

Another difficulty in making comparisons over time is the degree to which a hidden, unmeasured economy existed before and after transition. Certain estimates have suggested that between one third and a half of the economy in command economies was a black economy of trades that were hidden from official statistics. As the transition process has gone ahead, these hidden areas have become more transparent and therefore distort the before and after comparisons.

Externalities and the quality of the environment are important when considering living standards, but they are difficult to measure at any time and it is not clear whether these things are improving, staying the same or getting worse over recent years.

A significant component of GDP figures comprises military and defence expenditure. The higher the proportion of income spent in this area, the lower the standards of living. During the transition process there has been a significant move away from the production of armaments and the maintenance of armed forces. The result will be an increase in living standards that is difficult to measure. Also, changes in working conditions and hours worked change living standards in a way that is difficult to measure. If people can produce the same amount of products in fewer hours worked, then the increase in leisure time will increase their standard of living.

As the transition economies have increased their trade with the rest of the world, so new and different products will have become available to their citizens. This increase in variety and quality of products will have changed living standards in a way that is difficult to measure.

Before the transition process started, the countries of eastern Europe arguably had relatively high standards in the provision of merit goods, such as education and health, and public goods, such as law and order, sanitation and street lighting. During the transition process, it seems that certain of these products, including law and order, education and health, have had fewer resources allocated to them and this may have its effect on living standards now and in the future.

The points set out above illustrate the considerable difficulty that exists in trying to compare the command economies of the past with the transition economies of the present day.

12/15 marks

e Both parts of question 3 achieve maximum quality of language marks. A few marks are lost through lack of detail in part (i) and in part (ii) because the evaluative comment expected in a 'to what extent' answer is not fully developed.

Scored 51/60 = 85% = Grade A

Potential errors and omissions

(1) (i)
- Ignoring the word 'illustrate' and failing to include a diagram.
- Poor labelling of the diagram.
- Writing about supply and demand and forgetting to focus on the interaction of these two variables as the determinant of wages.

(ii) The question asks for an explanation of the potential market failures; it is not therefore necessary to analyse the results of implementing mandates.

(iii)
- The emphasis is on low-wage markets, not all labour markets.
- Failing to identify the difference between 'short term' and 'longer term'.

(2)
- The euro zone does not include all the countries of the EU.
- The question must be answered from the perspective of the producer, not the consumer.

(3) (i) The focus of the student should only be on the process of change from a command economy to a market economy and how it has been undertaken to eliminate the disadvantages of the old system and embrace the anticipated advantages of the new system.

(ii) Do not ignore 'to what extent', which requires evaluative comment.

Time allowed: 1 hour 45 minutes

A copy of the pre-issued case study is included with the question paper. All your answers should be in continuous prose; they will be assessed on the quality of the written language.

Total marks allocated: 60.

(1) With reference to extracts 1 and 2:

(i) Explain, using supply and demand curves, the problems caused by minimum price guarantees for EU farm products. (10 marks)

(ii) 'Arguably, the agricultural industry should be allowed to function under the same system as all other industries in a customs union, but with approved policies managed by national governments to stabilise farm incomes.' Assess this statement. (10 marks)

(2) Using extracts 3 and 4, examine the similarities and differences in the monetary policy of the Bank of England and the European Central Bank. (20 marks)

(3) With reference to extracts 5, 6 and 7, discuss whether the UK should adopt the euro as legal tender. (20 marks)

Mark scheme

(1) (i) To achieve full marks the candidate needs to recognise that minimum price guarantees cause a significant problem when they are set above the market clearing price. Using a diagram to illustrate the production of a surplus, the following problems need to be addressed:

- storage costs
- destroying the surplus
- whether to sell or give away the surplus outside the market
- consumers paying above the world price
- inefficient allocation of resources
- subsidised export prices and import levies damaging to farmers outside the EU

(10 marks. If no diagram is included, then mark out of 7.)

(ii) It will need to be recognised that a customs union functions with free trade inside the union and a common external tariff. This will lead to greater efficiency as resources are reallocated between farms, as illustrated by the theory of comparative advantage. The price mechanism would be used to clear markets, and import levies and export subsidies would be abolished. However, bearing in mind the peculiar problems of variable supply in the agricultural industry, individual governments would be able to stabilise incomes as long as they did not interfere with the market price. Also, the government could apply variable levels of income support to deal with perceived regional problems (10).

(2) Expect an explanation of monetary policy and an examination of most of the following similarities and differences.

Similarities

- Both policies are controlled by independent central banks.
- Their aim is to achieve monetary stability and price stability.
- Neither has targets for their foreign exchange rates.
- The main method of control is through short-term interest rates.
- Both aim for low, stable interest rates.
- Each manages its respective economy's liquidity.
- Both have targeted inflation and aim to foster economic growth.

(10 marks)

Differences

- The Bank of England (B of E) controls one country and the European Central Bank (ECB) controls 12.
- Different ways of providing information: the ECB uses the President's statement while the B of E publishes minutes from the Monetary Policy Committee (MPC) meetings.
- The Chancellor of the Exchequer can override B of E decisions.
- The ECB sets a target for M3 growth.
- Slightly different ways of operating in the open market for securities.
- B of E target for inflation is 2.5% or less for RPIX, whereas the ECB target is an average of 2.0% for the euro zone, using a 'Harmonised Index of Consumer Prices'.
- B of E has a target variation for inflation of ±1%, whereas the ECB is to be below 2%.

(10 marks)

Use the split 12/8 if the answer is unbalanced between similarities and differences.

(3) This is a discussion and therefore the answer needs to be balanced for and against joining the euro before a conclusion draws together the thoughts of the candidate.

For

- No transaction costs for currency.
- No exchange rate risk.
- A single currency will remove artificial barriers created by exchange rate fluctuations.
- No speculation on the movement of individual currencies.
- Certainty on agreed future prices in the euro area.
- Agreed target of low inflation and low interest rates which create an environment for economic growth.
- Increased competition, fewer restrictive practices.

(9 marks)

Against

- Transaction costs are negligible.
- Price stability is not guaranteed under a single currency.
- Euro exchange rate has been variable and less stable than that of the pound.
- Loss of control over domestic monetary policy and severe restrictions on fiscal policy.
- Business cycles are not synchronised.
- Significant discrepancy between present interest rates in the UK and in the euro zone.

(9 marks)

Use the split 10/8 rather than 9/9 if the answer is unbalanced between both sides of the argument, but save 2 marks for a conclusion to the discussion.

Response to paper 2: grade A answer

(1) (i) Minimum price guarantees have little effect if the market price is above the floor placed under agricultural prices. However, it is likely that, under pressure from political lobbies, the minimum price is set at a level that will protect the less efficient farmer and this price is likely to be above the equilibrium that would be established in a free market.

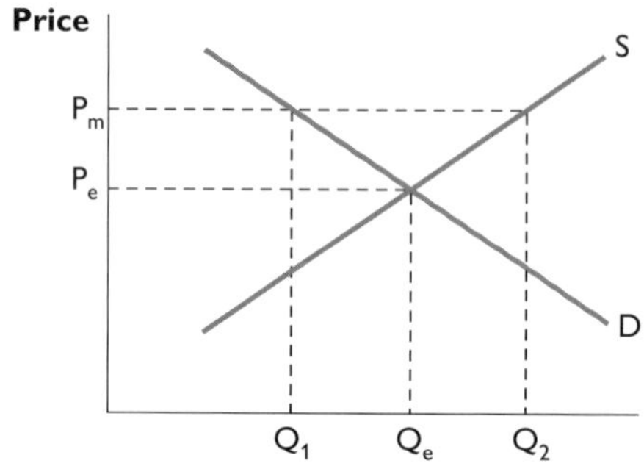

In the diagram above, a market equilibrium would be established at P_eQ_e. If the minimum price guarantee was P_m, then Q_2 would be supplied by farmers and Q_1 would be demanded by consumers, producing a surplus in the market. Ideally, this surplus would be stored for one or several years and then be released onto the market when the equilibrium price rises above P_m and a shortage develops. However, the evidence in the past from products like wine, beef and butter is that these surpluses build up year after year and cause significant problems, not the least of which is the cost of storage. This leads to further problems about whether the surplus should be destroyed, sold outside the market at a subsidised price which may damage foreign farmers, or given away to countries suffering from malnutrition and famine. Even this causes problems as farmers in these countries may lose their livelihood.

Overall, the system causes an inefficient allocation of resources, involves a bureaucracy to manage it and causes the consumer in the EU to face prices that are higher than world prices.

9/10 marks

e A good explanation with a wide range of problems identified, although they were not always fully developed.

(ii) Once a country joins a customs union, then it agrees to free trade, without tariffs, quotas and other trade restrictions, with all the other countries in the union. As a group of countries, the union may be protected from trade originating outside the union by the common external tariff. In the case of the European Union, this was set at a level that reflected the lower end of the existing tariffs around individual countries.

This means that all the firms and industries within the customs union compete freely with one another and comparative advantage should determine which firms flourish and expand and which decline and fail. However, in the case of the European Union the agricultural industry was made a special case because of the peculiar problems associated with unanticipated variable output and the swings in profitability from high prices and excessive profits to low prices and bankruptcies.

Minimum price guarantees and other protective measures created security for farm incomes and a constant supply of products. However, significant problems were inherent in a system that was trying to replace market forces, and the question that needs to be asked is whether it would be possible to support farm incomes and allow market forces to allocate resources.

If the agricultural industry was treated like other industries in the EU, there would be no control over prices and market forces would clear markets, removing the potential for surpluses and shortages. The common external tariff could be used to offer a measure of protection to farmers, but basically within the union they would be competing with one another for the best markets.

If it was felt that there should be support for farm incomes, then the governments of individual countries could directly support farm incomes without distorting prices. Although this interference would have a small distorting effect on the market, it would be very little compared with the problems currently manifesting themselves under the Common Agricultural Policy.

The changes suggested above would open up the agricultural industry to further international competition and there would be a transition period of considerable change within the industry as competition and comparative advantage bring about a reallocation of resources. However, over the longer term, more competition in the agricultural industry should bring about a more efficient allocation of scarce resources.

7/10 marks

e The request to examine the statement requires more than just explaining the statement. There is a brief attempt to look at the advantages of the CAP, but the answer predominantly supports the statement and is therefore unbalanced.

(2) Monetary policy and fiscal policy are the two main ways that the government pursues its macroeconomic policy, the objectives of which are full employment, stable prices, a sound balance of payments and economic growth.

Monetary policy is concerned with the way in which interest rates and money supply are manipulated to manage the overall level of aggregate monetary demand. In the UK this policy is pursued by an independent Bank of England (B of E), and in the euro zone this policy is managed by an independent European Central Bank (ECB).

As well as their independence from political overlords, both the ECB and B of E aim to achieve monetary stability and price stability and neither has an overt policy towards maintaining a particular rate of exchange for the currency they manage. Although a range of policies are available to both banks, they currently target short-term interest rates by intervention buying and selling of government securities on a daily basis. It is the responsibility of the B of E to manage liquidity in the UK so that there is sufficient currency to support the required liquidity position of the commercial banks. The ECB must act in a similar way. Both central banks aim to maintain low and stable rates of interest as well as a low and stable rate of inflation. Both of these targets are part of a policy to maintain a stable competitive environment from which the respective economies can produce a sustainable rate of economic growth. The low rates of interest have the effect of boosting investment and stimulating aggregate demand.

Since its inception in 1694, the Bank of England has been concerned with managing the monetary policy of one country, the United Kingdom. The ECB did not become active until 1999, more than 300 years later, when it was set up to manage the monetary policy of the 11 countries (now 12) which tied their currency irrevocably to the euro and are therefore known as the euro zone countries. Although they meet to discuss policy and set interest rates once a month, the ECB provides information through a presidential address, while the B of E publishes minutes taken at the Monetary Policy Committee meetings. In the case of the ECB, no one country can override any of its decisions, but in the UK, the Chancellor of the Exchequer has ultimate responsibility, and if the inflation target deviates more than 1% either side of its target, the Governor of the B of E must write an open letter to the Chancellor, and the Treasury can give instructions to the B of E for a limited period of time.

In the UK, specific monetary aggregates are monitored by the B of E. These include M0, which is referred to as narrow money (cash), and a broad money aggregate, M4. There is, however, no targeting in the UK, whereas the ECB sets a target for the growth of its M3 monetary aggregate. Also, the ECB has a slightly different approach to the way it operates in the open market for securities. The last main difference between the ECB and the B of E is the inflation targets that have been established. In the UK, the target is 2.5% for RPIX (excludes mortgage interest payments) with a target of variation of ±1%, whereas the ECB has targeted 2% or below. The UK has achieved its target over the last few years, although the ECB missed its target when inflation rose to above 2%.
17/20 marks

e The answer covers all the important points, although the examination of differences is more detailed than the cursory description of similarities. The structure of the answer is good as it clearly separates the similarities from the differences and precedes this with an explanation of monetary policy.

(3) Conversion to a European currency unit started in January 1999 for 11 of the 15 countries that make up the European Union. Each domestic currency was fixed irrevocably against the euro, and by 2002 domestic currencies will disappear and the euro will be the only legal tender in the euro zone. The UK was one of four countries which did not join the monetary union, although the UK government has promised its citizens a referendum on whether or not to join the euro belatedly.

Supporters of the euro point out that there will be significant gains for UK businesses as well as individuals through the removal of the transaction costs of trading currency. Also, prices will become more transparent, making comparisons easy throughout the euro zone. It will no longer be possible for countries to manipulate artificial protection through selling their currency to achieve a lower value. Individuals travelling through Europe will not have to change currencies and any purchases using a credit card will have their price fixed in euros. The certainty over prices agreed in the present for delivery in the future will also be of significant benefit to businesses that will not find their anticipated profits being reduced by a depreciating currency. Another direct effect of joining the euro is that there will no longer be flows of speculative money balances distorting currencies in anticipation of favourable movements in their price. This may, however, still go on between the euro and other currencies like the dollar.

An indirect benefit of joining the euro zone is the aim of the ECB to pursue low stable rates of inflation and interest, following the model developed in the German Central Bank (Bundesbank). Although the B of E is pursuing similar policies, it has not had a record of success in controlling either its rate of inflation or the rate of interest. Low and stable rates of inflation and interest are now considered to be the optimum conditions for producing economic growth. Overall, the single currency in a single market is likely to produce increased competition and greater efficiency.

Opponents of joining the single currency highlight the insignificance of transaction costs and the ease with which currencies can be traded in a free market. They also point out that price stability is not guaranteed under a single currency and that a committee of 11 or more countries making monetary decisions is not likely to pursue a policy that produces low inflation if the majority of the opinion supports expanding monetary demand.

Since the beginning of 1999 to the present day, the exchange rate of the euro against foreign currencies has fallen lower and been more variable than has the sterling exchange rate. The question is: what is the correct rate to fix for sterling against the euro? Too high and our exporters will be permanently disadvantaged; too low and inflationary pressures may be released in the UK economy.

Probably the single most important argument used against aligning sterling with the euro is the Bank of England's loss of control over manipulating monetary demand through adjustments to the money supply and interest rates. This would be a particular problem if the UK was expanding too fast while the other countries in Europe were entering a recession. The majority would push for expansionary monetary policies, which would be the wrong policy for the UK. Only if all business cycles throughout Europe were synchronised would a centralised policy be equally successful in all countries.

16/20 marks

A very good answer which takes a balanced look at the perceived advantages of joining or not joining the single European currency. It is well written and achieves the maximum quality of language marks. However, the one weakness that loses marks is the lack of a conclusion to the discussion. The student is asked to 'discuss' whether the UK should adopt the euro and the answer therefore needs a final paragraph which makes an evaluation of the relevant points and a judgement based on the evidence.

Scored 49/60 = 81.7% = Grade A

Potential errors and omissions

(1) (i)
- Because of the wording of the question, it is essential to include a diagram.
- A common mistake is to assume that the use of minimum prices is the same as prices fixed too high or too low relative to the equilibrium price. Remember that the market will only be distorted if the minimum price is set at a level which is *above* equilibrium.

(ii)
- 'Assess this statement' requires a little more to the answer than just an explanation of the statement. It is necessary to comment on the relevance and correctness of the statement.
- It is important to recognise that farm incomes can be stabilised without price intervention.

(2)
- Avoid the mistake of describing the policy and role of the B of E and ECB without making comparative statements.
- Clearly separate the similarities from the differences.

(3) For the answer to qualify as a 'discussion', there must be at least two points of view and a conclusion in which you can express your own preference.

Time allowed: 1 hour 45 minutes

A copy of the pre-issued case study is included with the question paper. All your answers should be in continuous prose; they will be assessed on the quality of the written language.

Total marks allocated: 60.

(1) Using extract 1:

(i) Analyse the relationship between the changes in real GDP and inflation in Russia between 1990 and 1999. (6 marks)

(ii) Explain what is meant by a budget deficit and why Russia is trying to reduce the size of its deficit as a proportion of its GDP. (6 marks)

(iii) Using supply and demand curves, explain how, in a free market, a country's exchange rate is determined. (8 marks)

(2) (i) The introduction of the euro is described in extract 2 as having many 'spillover' benefits. Explain, with examples, what is meant by a spillover benefit. (10 marks)

(ii) Extract 2 provides a one-sided description of the external benefits that may be derived from 'economic and monetary union'. Can you identify any potential external costs from establishing a single currency within the European Union? (5 marks)

(3) Using all the available information and your own knowledge of the situation, discuss whether the introduction of the euro will help promote economic growth in all the EU countries and the other countries of Europe. (25 marks)

Mark scheme

(1) (i) This answer requires a description of the changes in real GDP and inflation, with particular attention given to the main break in trend. The student is expected to notice the degree to which there is an inverse relationship between the relevant changes (4). For full marks the answer requires some reasoning to explain the relationship (2).

(ii) An explanation of a budget deficit, including detail from the relevant extract (3) and some points to say why Russia is aiming to reduce its size:

- given a primary surplus of 3%, a significant proportion of government expenditure is on interest charges
- to produce a sustainable fiscal policy
- to avoid crowding out private investment
- to remove some of the strain on monetary policy
- to help bring down the rate of inflation

(3 marks)

(iii) A clearly labelled diagram with another currency on the vertical axis to determine a price and the quantity of the currency under consideration on the horizontal axis (3). An explanation of the demand and supply curves (5).

(2) (i) The explanation of a spillover benefit as an external benefit to society which is not paid for (4). The examples may include:
- removal of transaction costs
- removal of exchange rate risk
- increase in output and real income
- lower interest rates with greater stability and less interest rate risk
- higher investment
- greater exchange rate stability
- overall increase in efficiency
- more countries holding euro balances
- synchronisation of business cycles

(6 marks)

(ii) Expect some of the following:
- difficulty in becoming accustomed to the new currency
- costs of repricing
- loss of national control over money supply and interest rates
- damage to the economy if agreed at too high a rate
- inability to respond to domestic problems by manipulating aggregate monetary demand

(5 marks)

(3) A clear explanation of what is meant by economic growth (4). Also expect that there will be a discussion around three groupings of countries:
- euro zone countries (7)
- EU countries not in the euro zone (7)
- other central and eastern European countries, including the transitional economies (7)

For these groupings, split the 7 marks approximately 4/3 between points of agreement and disagreement over the promotion of economic growth.

Response to paper 3: grade A answer

(1) (i) Figure 1 illustrates the relationship between the changes in real GDP and the rate of inflation. In general terms, the relationship can be described as inverse. Between 1990 and 1992 the rate of inflation begins to rise slowly and then accelerates to a peak of 1,500%. During the same years the real GDP falls from –4% to –14% per annum. Between 1992 and 1999 the rate of inflation falls quickly and then gradually to a low of 57.1% in the year up to October 1999. Although there are a number of breaks in trend, the general movement is for the GDP contraction to decelerate, moving above zero by 1999. Overall, it seems that GDP fell rapidly when inflation accelerated and then began to decelerate slowly when the rate of inflation fell. It seems that high rates of inflation are damaging to the growth in real GDP and low rates of inflation are conducive to a positive growth in real GDP.

5/6 marks

The description of the relevant changes is good, particularly as the student notices that the fall in inflation causes a deceleration in the rate of fall in real GDP. A common mistake is to misread the vertical axis and refer to a rise in real GDP. However, the explanation is brief and only scores 1 mark out of a possible 2. It would have been relevant to point out that other economic variables could be having an effect on either inflation or real GDP.

(ii) A budget deficit occurs when the yearly government expenditure is greater than the revenue received from taxation. For the period from January to September of 1999 the Russian deficit was 62.7 billion roubles. This was estimated at 3.5% of GDP, which was a fall from 4.4% the previous year. An important reason for reducing the size of the budget deficit is the amount of interest payments on debt. It is suggested that, without interest payments, the budget would be in a surplus of 3%. Also, selling government debt requires interest rates to be higher and this may crowd out private sector investment. A smaller deficit or its removal is more likely to produce a sustainable fiscal policy with lower inflation and higher growth rates.

6/6 marks

The candidate clearly understands deficit and makes some relevant suggestions as to why Russia wants to reduce the size of the deficit.

(iii)

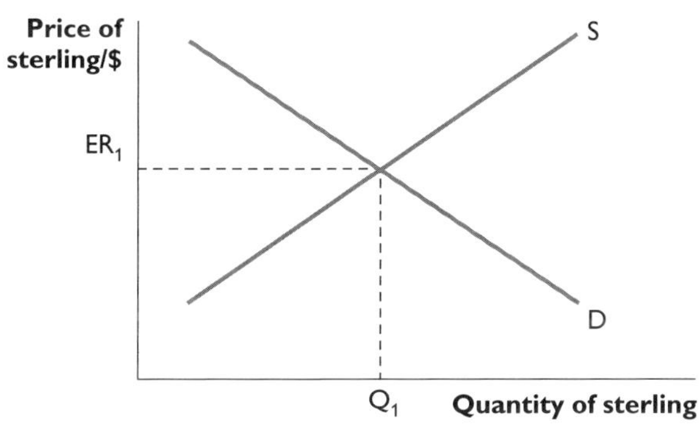

The equilibrium price of sterling is, in the example above, measured in dollars and occurs where the demand curve for sterling intersects the supply curve. The demand for sterling is determined by the demand by foreigners for UK exports. As the price of sterling falls, so foreigners will find that the sterling price of UK products falls and they will demand more products (sterling). The supply of sterling is determined by UK demand for imports. As the price of sterling rises, so the price of imports falls, and, if the demand for imports is elastic, then more sterling will be supplied to buy more foreign products. The result will be an equilibrium at ER_1 where Q_1 of sterling is demanded by foreigners and supplied by the UK.

8/8 marks

A good answer with a clear diagram.

(2) (i) A spillover or neighbourhood effect is an uncontracted cost or benefit on the community caused by the production or consumption of a product. The cost or benefit is not paid for by those members of society who are damaged or those who benefit from the product in question. In this case, the introduction of the euro is described as having benefits to society as a whole. These are usually referred to as external benefits and differ from private benefits which are paid for by the user.

Businesses in Europe will benefit from the introduction of the euro because they will no longer have to pay transaction costs to buy other currencies. This will also remove the risk of exchange rates moving unfavourably and unpredictably, and because costs will generally be lower, output and real income is likely to rise.

Another benefit that will directly be felt by the consumer is when they go on holiday or travel in Europe. They will not have to fill their wallets and purses with many different currencies as the euro will suffice.

Alongside the introduction of the euro is a policy to keep interest rates low and stable throughout the euro zone. This will give businesses confidence to increase investment, expand, take advantage of economies of scale and increase efficiency in a competitive single market.

Finally, because all countries in the euro zone are faced with the same currency and low interest rates it is likely that business cycles will be synchronised and smoothing policies will be effective throughout Europe.

All of the points described above are possible benefits that the user will not pay for when domestic currencies are replaced by a single currency.

8/10 marks

e 4/4 for explanation of a spillover benefit and 4/6 for the examples.

(ii) The immediate effect of introducing a single currency is that consumers may be confused by the prices and no longer be able to compare relative prices efficiently. The older a person is, the greater the difficulty in adjusting to a new currency.

There will also be business costs involved in repricing products and potential problems for people trading in products which now have unfamiliar prices.

For the country as a whole, the loss of control over the money supply and interest rates may create difficulties when domestic economic activity requires an adjustment to interest rates or an increase in liquidity that is not felt throughout the rest of Europe.

4/5 marks

e One more external cost is needed for full marks.

(3) Economic growth is an increase in the productive capacity per person in an economy. It is recognised when the production possibility frontier (ppf) of an economy shifts outwards, as illustrated in the diagram opposite.

The ppf aa joins together all the possible combinations of consumer and capital goods that can be produced by the productive factors in an economy. If it shifts outwards to bb, this means that, given the same amount of resources, more can be produced. This is economic growth and it is characterised by higher real incomes.

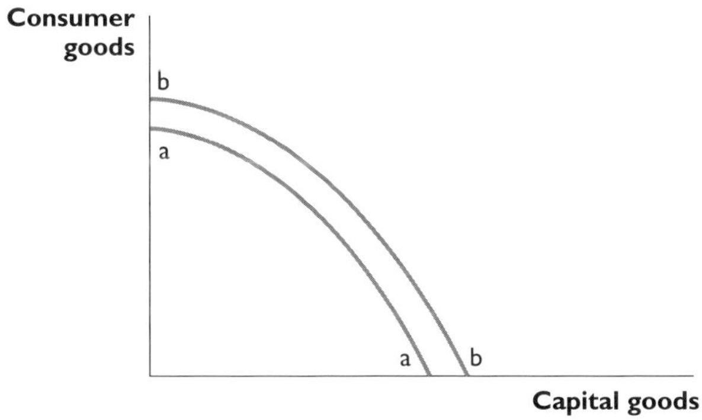

If all the countries in the euro zone start trading with a single currency, then they will find that their costs of production are lower through the removal of trading costs for currencies. Prices will also be more transparent and firms will be encouraged to expand in what is seen as a single, larger market. Low interest rates and increased investment are also characteristics associated with economic growth.

However, for economic growth to take place, many other factors must be considered, including changes in technology, invention and innovation, a mobile labour force and the acceptance of changes in working practices, to name but a few. Also, although economic growth may be achieved throughout the euro zone, on average there is no reason to believe that each country will benefit equally. For example, countries on the geographical fringe may find that new capital investment is drawn to the centre of the market and, now they can no longer protect themselves by an international frontier, their economies may undergo negative growth.

At present there are three EU countries (UK, Denmark and Sweden) that have not adopted the euro. Obviously, they will not benefit directly from the introduction of the currency as described above. However, if the single market expands, then these countries can expect to grow as there are higher real incomes in the EU and therefore increased demand for all its products. Over the long term, these countries may lose out if they do not attract the new investment that prefers to locate in the euro zone. In contrast these outsiders could benefit from being able to manage their own monetary and fiscal policies without the restrictions that would be imposed upon them by being part of the euro zone.

For the rest of Europe, including the independent states of Central and Eastern Europe (CEE) and the Commonwealth of Independent States (CIS), there may be some indirect benefits from the faster growth rate in the EU. As real incomes grow inside the union, so there will be a bigger market for the products for which CIS and CEE countries have comparative advantage. In addition, they may benefit from cheaper foodstuffs as the agricultural surpluses of the EU are sold at subsidised prices outside their union. Alternatively, their own farming industry may be damaged. Finally, the faster rates of growth in the EU countries may damage the other European countries if they become more efficient at producing products that were traditionally made outside their national boundaries.

As has been discussed, the introduction of the euro may have both positive and negative effects throughout Europe.

19/25 marks

e A good attempt at dealing with the issue across Europe. Although it was weak, the candidate did try to produce a conclusion to the discussion. The answer achieved all the quality of language marks available in the mark scheme. The distribution of marks was 4/4, 6/7, 5/7 4/7 (see mark scheme).

Scored 50/60 = 83.3% = Grade A

Potential errors and omissions

(1) (i) • Note that the lowest recorded rate of inflation is still very high, i.e. 57.1%.
• Note that changes in real GDP are all negative over the whole period except for the 1999 forecast.

(ii) Refer to what is included in extract 1, but do not be limited to just this in your search for an answer.

(iii) • Marks will be lost if a clearly labelled diagram is not included.
• On the diagram you can only measure the price of one currency by using another currency; therefore if you are measuring sterling, on the vertical axis you will need to use dollars, euros or some other currency.

(2) (i) Refer to external benefits only. No marks will be allocated for external costs.

(ii) Refer to external costs only. No marks will be allocated for external benefits.

(3)
- A discussion must include contrasting views regarding the relationship between introducing the euro and economic growth.
- Do not misread the question and only refer to the euro zone countries. The question is also asking you to cover EU countries not in the euro zone and the other countries of Europe.